LEARNING TO READ AND SPELL

LEARNING TO READ AND SPELL:
The Child's Knowledge of Words

Edmund H. Henderson

Northern Illinois University Press □ DeKalb, Illinois

Edmund H. Henderson is Director of the McGuffey Reading Center and Professor
of Education, University of Virginia, Charlottesville, Virginia.

Library of Congress Cataloging in Publication Data

Henderson, Edmund H.
   Learning to read and spell.

   Bibliography: p.
   1. Reading. 2. English language—Orthography
and spelling. 3. Spelling ability. I. Title.
LB1050.H428   372.4   81–14117
ISBN 0−87580−078−5   AACR2
ISBN 0−87580−526−4 (pbk.)

Dedicated to

Margaret Hardcastle Henderson

Contents

Acknowledgments

If this book has merit, it should be considered due primarily to the inspiration and scholarly help I have received from the following remarkable students. Each of us in turn is grateful for the opportunity we have had to work at a place of great beauty and academic encouragement, the University of Virginia.

William Barnes	Joy Harris
Sheila Barry Barton	Patricia B. Kenyon
Donald Bear	Mary Jane Kita
James W. Beers	Betty Lee
Paula Cooper	Darrell Morris
Eugenia Ing Fisher	Robert Schlagal
Ann Fordham	Elizabeth Stever
Richard Gentry	Susan Stonecash
Charlene Gill	Charles Temple
Thomas Gill	William Shane Templeton
Jean Wallace Gillet	Jerome Zutell
George Graham	

LEARNING TO READ AND SPELL

Introduction 1

For over 100 years the major debate about reading instruction has centered on a single question. How is it that children learn English words? Some have argued that words are best learned as wholes in relation to pictures or in the context of a sentence. It has been held by others that children should first learn letters, then letter patterns and the sounds associated with these. While nearly all have agreed that the purpose of reading is to comprehend, there have been sharp differences of opinion about the priorities given to comprehension instruction versus that applied to the mastery of basic word knowledge.

Throughout this 100-year period our efforts to understand word knowledge proceeded on the basis of an adult analysis of written English as if it were a code. It was assumed that there is a relatively simple bond between speech and print and that its form was such that it could be described straightforwardly by logic. Reading methodologists thus focused on only two dimensions of the problem: (1) the logical relations between spoken and written language, and (2) the effects of one program of instruction as contrasted with those of another.

Conspicuously absent both in basic research and in the methodological argument was a curiosity about the child himself as a learner. Regardless of what a surface analysis seemed to suggest, and regardless of the effects of teaching by one plan or another, this critical question lay dormant and unexplored. What do children know about written language as they progress toward literacy?

In the early 1960s Noam Chomsky's theoretical focus on language competence led researchers to examine the phenomena of oral language acquisition from this different point of view. As a result, those quaint and familiar patterns of children's language have been shown to form a grammatical progression far more elegant and natural than could possibly have been construed from a surface analysis alone. This line of research inspired our efforts to study children's acquisition of knowledge about written English in a similar way.

No student of reading instruction can doubt that words may be learned as wholes or that they may be analyzed into elements and even, after a fashion, constructed synthetically. Insofar as spelling is concerned, it is beyond question that words can be memorized serially by letter sequence and that ultimately many are produced quite automatically by motor response. On the other hand it is equally clear that such conceptualizations of word knowledge are incomplete. They will not serve to explain, for example, the ability of a child to spell nonsense words correctly or the power of the literate speller to command a writing vocabulary of 70,000 words. Thus it would seem that the endless arguments about reading methodology have endured not because either side was right or wrong but because neither had achieved an adequate perspective of the problem as a whole.

It is now ten years since my students and I embarked on our study of children's knowledge of words. We did not know then exactly how to proceed, but we felt very sure that some better understanding of this matter could and should be reached. Our hypothesis was a simple one. We believed that one important aspect of children's word knowledge was conceptual and that these concepts would change and expand progressively over the years. We believed further that we would be able to infer what these understandings were by studying the errors that children made when they attempted to spell words they did not know.

To have a hunch about something important and a belief, however uncertain, that it can be tested is to know adventure in a very pure form. The excitement of the problem has stayed with us and seen us through many days of work. It has led my students into new and demanding subjects where they have labored both to learn and to teach me. We have wandered and wavered many times in our efforts, as ever must be the case when curiosity leads one back again to study in new disciplines. Yet the importance of the educational question has remained, as has our belief that it was we as teachers, rather than the substantive scientist, who must take the responsibility for asking a question of this kind. By degrees and by good fortune we began to find our way, and now at long last I believe that we have something positive and practical to say about the teaching of reading and writing. To do so is the purpose of this book.

Sharing Educational Research

Our research interest continues, but now our goals are ranging a little wider. We wish to see if we can find progressive patterns of word knowledge cross-culturally and from these tease out perhaps some general principles about written language. This work is now happily under way. Still at this point we have in hand a reasonably convincing series of developmental studies, and we find these data very helpful to us as we teach children in clinic and classroom settings. Thus, I feel that the time has come to present our findings. Educational research proceeds in a manner quite different from the "pure sciences." Whereas researchers in the other sciences derive the problem from a theory based on previously presented data of scientists in their fields, our approach to the problem of learning to read and spell derives from a fundamental perplexity that we find in the actual act of teaching children. And just as the formula for deriving a problem in the "pure sciences" is well established, so too are the formulae for presentation of the findings. However, in the presentation of the material derived from a study based on educational research, the method of presentation and evaluation of the data collected are not nearly as well established or fixed.

In the course of our work we are constantly setting children to tasks of various kinds. These derive in part from theory and in part from tradition—the received knowledge of experience. We do of course have expectations that what we teach will result in a growth of competence on the part of our pupils. Nearly always many do learn and so strengthen our confidence in our method. But also some do fail and force us to wonder why. Is it want of heed or industry by us or by the child? Is it perhaps genetic or caused by some obscure physiological abnormality? From time to time, however, we arrive at an even more troublesome quandary. We begin to wonder if what we teach, that is, what we have children do, really is related, or as directly related as it should be, to what we expect them to learn or be able to do? Put simply, we wonder if we know what we are talking about.

It is from such doubts as these that true educational questions arise. We must search through the tangle of action and reaction, task and product, until we can find both the problem itself and a way to shed some better light on it. It follows then that the role of educational research is not one that tests the boundaries of an abstract theory. Instead, we but use theory and such investigative techniques as we can find to gain some focus on the complicated things that teachers and pupils do.

The proof or value of educational research lies not in its implication for theory but for practice. The studies themselves, of course, must be just—honestly posed, reproducible, and generalizable, but they must in addition have a fairly high degree of ecological validity. Findings must apply to real not to staged conditions. They must be informative, but they need not, indeed should not, be prescriptive, for as James correctly observed long ago, teaching itself is an art that must at each instance advance by means of teachers who exercise their own creative faculties (James 1899, p. 24).

Concerns such as these have guided the plan I have adopted in reporting our studies of children's advancing concepts about the form of English words. Our work began from a genuine perplexity that I felt about what we taught and what was learned in current programs of reading and spelling instruction. Moreover, these doubts did not come about suddenly but gradually as I studied the subject intensively for many years.

It seemed to me that if I were to present the problem clearly it would be necessary to sketch in a brief history of reading instruction, showing the forms it has taken and the forces that have molded it to its present status. In addition, I wished to show my own perspective of these conditions and the teaching strategies that I followed before the present work began. Such is the content of Chapter 2. Its primary goal is to show the emergence of a question for educational research. I hope also, however, that it will prove a useful exercise in thinking about our teaching practices and indeed in challenging their validity.

In Chapter 3, I have presented the background for our word research, and in Chapter 4 the specific studies themselves. I have tried to describe the work as it evolved and to fill in by degrees those theoretical ideas that made it possible. My effort throughout has been that of any interpretive writer, to tell enough but not more than the reader wished to know. If I have erred somewhat in the latter, the error must be seen to stem from my enthusiasm for the topic and the sure knowledge that it is this work that has made our more recent pedagogical insights possible.

Chapters 5 and 6 deal with the teaching of reading and writing and cover that progression from preschool to the high school years. Here my aim is to show in fact that the findings of our studies do serve us in the daily work of teaching children to read and write. As argued earlier, I view this kind of explication an absolutely necessary component in any serious account of educational research. Findings that float free or hark back only to theory are insufficient. We must translate these into actions that may be taken by any sensible teacher, each in his own way.

Unfortunately, whenever one writes directly about teaching, the implication may be that a final method has been declared. Nothing could be further from the truth for what is presented in this book. My aim is to illustrate, not to prescribe. Those things that my students and I do today as teachers are limited by our own resources. If we live and practice our art, they will change and, I hope, improve tomorrow.

On the other hand, what we do as teachers is not done whimsically. We do study children intently, think about what they know and try to gear our actions to their various capacities and dispositions. In this sense what is described in Chapters 5 and 6 is intended to be directly informative. Specifically, I hope to show that an understanding of what children know about written language does make possible more sensitive and more effective teaching options.

In Chapter 7, I have turned the focus of our work to that broad area variously known as reading or learning disability. This has come about because I have worked almost daily with such problems for the past twenty-five years, first at the University of Delaware and presently at the University of Virginia. At both centers our major interest and commitment has been to reading and writing instruction in the broadest possible context. We have continued to find, however, that a careful study of what has gone wrong for some children is a rich source of information about how to make it go right for many. In addition, we have found that teaching children who labor under difficulties is a powerful stimulus to the refinement of our basic teaching skills.

What we have learned about children's knowledge of words has proved particularly helpful in dealing with special cases of reading disability. All children make errors of certain kinds when they attempt to spell words they do not know, and these errors, as will be shown, fall into predictable categories as a consequence of the child's age and learning experience. Thus, it has become possible to distinguish between errors of this kind—"normal errors"—and those that deviate from the norm. The identification of these "deviant errors" has come to serve us very well as a qualitative diagnostic tool. Further, it has offered some effective implications for instruction, both special and general. A report of these ideas is our concern in Chapter 7.

So it turns out that the heaviest emphasis of this report, the greatest length and detail, is devoted to the application of our findings to the decision we make when teaching children to read and write. I believe firmly that it should be thus in any serious work in education.

Some Thoughts on the Reading Process

When one meets a teaching problem, it is inevitable that theory will raise its head. It was Chomsky's model of language competence, in fact, that suggested to us a new way of coming to a better understanding of what children know about written English. In the course of our studies this competence model has influenced our thinking about reading and learning to read in a surprising way.

Long ago, Huey (1908) employed a metaphor to describe those aspects of text perception that he could not then address empirically. He said that reading is always a projection outward from the mind, where mind both serves as light and screen (p. 106). This led him to assert that meaningful substitutions in the course of reading were a sign of strength rather than weakness (p. 349). Such "errors" seemed evidence that the reader was using his full mind to gain efficiency in the act of word or phrase identification. For many years I accepted this position almost without question.

Now it seems to me that Huey's metaphor goes too far. Obviously, a mistake in word identification is a mistake no matter how well motivated and "sensible" the error is. The same must be said for errors in spelling as well. Competency must result in accuracy, not error. If the mind constructs things incorrectly, then the mind has interfered.

From such considerations I have come to believe that text perception must function to some degree independently of overt propositional thought. Clearly, knowledge of the world in general, including what we know about reading, must govern the reading act in many important ways. But it need not, and I think more probably does not, govern the perceptual act itself in reading. Instead I am inclined now to view text perception as cognitive in form—tacit and unique in its relation to language. I believe its function to be automatic, direct, and unmediated by conscious thought, though modified and refined by experience with written language.

To some it may seem that this change of perspective is quite radical, but I think of it as an extension of my former views, not a shift to another position. When reading is viewed from the perspective of performance, then Huey's metaphor, or its modern equivalent, the constructivist or "top down" models, apply with good force (Goodman 1976; F. Smith 1971, for example.) On the other hand, when one considers the reader's competence at the moment of fixation or the moment of writing a word, then a design like that of Gough (1972) or LaBerge and Samuels (1974) seems more telling.

Ultimately some accommodation must be reached. Clearly, progress is being made by those who are attempting to conceptualize the full cascading drama of thought in relation to language (De Beaugrande 1981). I think it will be necessary also, however, to rework our present assumptions about those events entailed in the perceptions of written language. To this end I think there is much in the historical record of language and in the more narrowly focused physiological models that will be helpful. I feel also that our studies may be usefully interpreted within this smaller frame. Doubtless, as Huey observed, some new light on these matters will resolve many differences among us that are now very probably more apparent than real (Huey 1908, p. 102).

A recent, very interesting work by Philip Lieberman (1975) argues that spoken language had its beginning in man at the vast distance of a million years ago. In contrast, written language, crude graphs representing a moon calendar, seems first to have emerged at about 40,000 B.C., and with this event a cultural flourishing among the human races can be seen. Thus, while modern writing is a relatively recent artifact, ca. 5,000 B.C., it must nonetheless have undergone a very long period of refinement. Such historical evidence tends to support a belief that human spoken language lies deep in our physical makeup and that written language is well shaped to its role.

There has not yet been, according to Eccles (1977), any detailed study of the physiological workings of the language area of the brain. There is, however, well over a hundred years of medical research which defines in some measure the differentiation of brain function (Geschwind 1974). Broca's area is crucial for syntactic form and is closely associated with the motor areas of articulation and speech. Wernicke's area serves the lexicon and is closely related to the hippocampus. All of these language centers have been found to operate autonomously, for when they are isolated by a lesion from those other areas which serve the functions of propositional thought, new messages can still be learned and old ones repeated on cue (Geschwind 1974). Equally remarkable is the fact that certain mongoloids can read English text verbatim—without having been taught to do so and without any comprehension of what they are saying signifies (Mehegan and Dreifuss 1972). Relatively recently, Geschwind (1974) has reported that the dominant language area is distinct by its larger size and is thus unilaterally a physical given. This finding has been corroborated in studies of fetuses and stillborn infants. Man alone is marked by this central feature.

It thus seems reasonable to assume that spoken language is a unique facet of man's intellectual competence and that it is bound up with and must interact with his management of artifacts, including written language. Higher animals do seem to "think"; clearly they have intentions and carry out strategies. But the chimpanzee does not generate language naturally, nor is he able to hurl a missile to a moving target. Man alone has the capacity to aim and simultaneously release the throwing action to that purpose. I am persuaded that human language functions in a similar manner.

There is little doubt in my mind that Noam Chomsky had a fair grasp of this physiological terrain as he advanced his model of language competence and worked out a mathematical scheme of syntactic and phonological rules. His plan to set language apart from the propositional force of thought appears to me well founded. It is in this particular sense that I have reached the conclusion that reading, too, in a narrow sense, is not "thinking." This is in no way to deny the significance of thought for language or the compatibility of language form as the servant of thought. It is simply to insist that a distinction be made between the two events. Reading, as a competence, must, I think, be defined within the limits of this dichotomy.

I recall many years ago a discussion about reading that took place between Hobart Mowrer and a distinguished gathering of scholars. These included, among others, David Russell, Sterle Artley, Arthur Gates, Russell Stauffer, and J. P. Guilford. The majority argued that reading was thinking, but Professor Mowrer stood his ground. Thinking, he said, was what that man was doing in the statue by Rodin (Le Penseur). Reading was different from that. At the time I thought him most arbitrary and difficult. Today, I believe that Professor Mowrer was entirely correct and that the distinction he asked us to make is absolutely necessary for a reasonable understanding of reading.

For a very long time we have attempted to explain how reading worked—and here I am thinking particularly about word identification—as if it were a kind of puzzle. It is in this sense that the term *decoding* is typically used. The assumption is that one learns the rules that order letter-sound relationships. Curiously, however, these rules seem always to express what one who knows words may *say* about them, in contrast to what one knows to *know* them in the first place. Our study of children's invented spelling suggests clearly that children's knowledge of words advances in a common conceptual progression that reflects a truly marvelous and abstract "sense" of alphabetic writing. This occurs almost independently of social background, dialect, or method of instruction.

I have been forced to conclude that the accommodation by young speakers to the written form of their language is, in essence, a profoundly natural set of events. This accommodation occurs because language is an autonomous central function to which written language has been shaped. Children appear not to require advice from thought in this matter, nor at present has "thought" sufficient knowledge to advise them.

This does not mean, of course, that reading is not learned or that it does not in most cases require the assistance of a teacher. It does imply, however, that the instructional goal must be to facilitate the accommodation rather than to reconstruct it artificially. My principal emphasis in Chapters 5 and 6 is to suggest some ways that this may be done.

If an accommodation is to be reached between language in its spoken and its written forms, it can be done in no other way, I think, than through experience with written language. This is the stuff that the language centers of the brain must feed on. If my view of reading is correct in this regard, good literature will facilitate learning; materials that are badly written will impede it.

While the Chomskian model of language competence may comport with the physiology of the brain, it has not proved very satisfactory when addressed to matters of language use. (Nor was it intended to do so.) This is so because *use* implies intention and the thrust of mind as a whole. A more recent movement in linguistics and psycholinguistics has centered on semantics or meaning as the base structure of language from which syntax and phonology are seen to derive directly. This work appears to me most valuable as it suggests those characteristics of thought that relate to and govern language use. It is suggestive as well, I think, about the manner in which the language function itself must have evolved. For my own part, however, I am still persuaded that proposition and speech should be separately construed.

When the distinction is made between language and thought, the primary role of language experience is clearly revealed. Revealed also is the tacit and automated character of the knowledge gained by this experience. The same distinction serves equally to highlight the role of thought in language use. We do not instruct our phrases how to form themselves but instead command them to a purpose. We are not invaded by the meanings of another but take from the flow of speech or the lines of print what we can or will. As one wag put it, "However else could so many speak so much nonsense, or we as listeners bear it without insult."

Free from the complex business of *making* language, thought may give it wings. Thought samples meaning in every way it wishes from surface sound to metaphor, from straight assertion to abstract formulation. It is free as well to forego all effort beyond a simple recognition or to disengage entirely and conduct a ratiocination of its own. Learning to use language efficiently and honestly, with a degree of rigor appropriate to purpose and with a purpose appropriate to one's responsible role in society, should be the major goal of instruction for the literate of every culture.

Just as we cannot specify the mechanistic skills of letter, word, and sentence recognition, those things accomplished by the language centers of the brain, so also are we unable to reduce the elements of thought to particles for practice. We can, however, exercise thought as it is addressed to language in every form and hold it to the highest standard of performance it can give. Such is the business of reading instruction throughout the grades.

To accomplish this educational goal, learners will need reading material that they can understand, which means simply that the material must be reasonably congruent with their language and world experience. In addition, they will need teachers who can activate the search for understanding and set standards of rigor and intent. None of this is likely to occur, I think, in a vacuum in which the process of reading is the single objective. Therefore, a curriculum that is socially and culturally alive must underlie all the instruction undertaken.

In summary then, how does reading seem to work? It is at first simply speaking to print in a crude and ill-adjusted way. By degrees it becomes a highly abstract and wonderfully accurate adjustment between that which the text affords and that which the plans for speech can generate. It is a thing that human beings learn to do, usually with the help of a literate adult. It can be accomplished because writing is age formed to the language capacities of the brain. Reading will occur when the learner is immersed in the medium of print, even though the precise properties of this accommodation are still unknown. It is for this reason that action must precede analysis in any pedagogical effort. Language and thought are dichotomous functions centrally, and this happy condition allows thought to command language in all its forms. Thus, beyond the overseeing of a material accommodation to written language, the major goal of reading instruction is to teach an intellectual command of language that is efficient and honest.

In Search of Method

If you listen to parents talking at PTA or coffee hour or under the beach umbrellas, you will learn much about what they as educational consumers believe to be true of the teaching of reading. It is overwhelmingly held, I think, that to read is a "good thing" and that to learn to read is crucial both socially and economically. It is thought that the earlier a child learns to read, the brighter he is, and that the outcomes of the kindergarten and first-grade years decree a sure prediction of success or life-long failure.

There is some truth in these convictions, but there also is some error, for the lines are too strictly drawn. Reading may be a good thing, but it may also be a stupid waste of time. Many bright children do learn to read early, but a good many average children do so too.

Most children do learn to read by age seven, but a goodly number of bright and average children do not learn rapidly until the age of eight or even nine. Fluent and versatile reading ability is most certainly a valuable asset for any man or woman, but only if it is employed wisely. Moreover, there are many successful people in our society today—and here I mean successful in both economic and in human terms—who read indifferently and spell wretchedly.

One major problem in reading education today is consumer fear— a fear that failure will reveal in children a want of intelligence and that gross illiteracy will doom them to poverty and ruin. A well-intentioned but alarmist press fans these fears, and so too, do the equally well-intentioned advertising agents for the publishers of reading programs and materials. It is, moreover, from these two sources that parents get most of their information about how reading should be taught—about what works and what fails in the classroom. Unfortunately, this information is incomplete, true only in part and therefore misleading.

I have found it to be held generally that there is a right way to teach reading and that one or another system, be it the old-fashioned way or the latest innovation, is "the solution" to our educational ills. The arguments swing back and forth: the school is too prescriptive; the school is too permissive. There is too much drill; the fundamentals are being neglected. More phonics should be taught; children should stop sputtering sounds and start reading books. The pattern of these charges and countercharges is as deadly and dead-ending as the "yes I am, no you're not" discussion of five year olds. Curiously and conspicuously absent is that more fundamental question: do we really know what children do as they learn to read? Common sense would assure us that there must indeed have been much good in the ancient ways of teaching reading, as well as some mischief and misconception. One could scarcely doubt that there must be some efficiency in certain aspects of most phonics programs and in the new linguistic approaches so popular today. Moreover, few of us would judge as adequate a school setting in which there were skills only and no books, no stories, and no material to discuss and write about.

We, as educators, need to address ourselves to an understanding of the reading process—insofar as we are able—and become informed about the history of teaching methodology. Only in this way, I think, will we be able to escape from the dreary repetition of teaching fads and perhaps begin to find some constants, that is, some sound and universal practices from which we may hope to build a more felicitous manner of teaching children to read. It is my hope that the work of my students and myself will be judged as a useful effort toward that end.

Reading and Spelling Instruction in Perspective

Reading Methodologies

☐ The Alphabet Method

Oldest of the reading methodologies is that called the Alphabet or ABCDery method. This approach was followed, in essence, in Greece and Rome and in schools of the Reformation and in Colonial America well into the early Constitutional days of our nation. In this plan, instruction was begun somewhere between the ages of five and seven and commenced with the teaching of the alphabet letters. Thereafter, words in familiar passages (such as homilies, prayers, or the like) were spelled out and learned until these texts could be recited correctly. In the New England hornbook a syllabary was added so that the common short vowel patterns (*ab, ib, ub, ob,* etc.) could also be memorized. From here the pupil moved to passages of decreasing familiarity, for example, from the Lord's Prayer, to the Catechism, to Genesis, until literacy was achieved. Typically, about three years were required to accomplish the task. Pupils bound toward a scholarly goal were then ready to begin reading the classics.

Most educators of the past century (see, for example, N. B. Smith 1965; Huey 1908) have had little good to say about the alphabet method. They have deplored the dull drilling of young children to learn their letters and the rote spelling out of words to name them. Huey, for example, wondered how in the world the naming of letters could assist in the "reading" of a word, though he guessed that it might be helpful for spelling. Many of us today who are accustomed to controlled readers and simple *"Cat-in-the-Hat"* vocabularies marvel at the terrible difficulty of the beginning passages used then.

On the other hand, it has always seemed to me that an approach that endured so long must have had some redeeming virtues, and it did. The difficulty of the passages was obviated by the fact that children in each culture already knew them by heart. Further, that the names of alphabet letters bear a profound and stable relation to the written word has been a major finding of our recent research (J. Beers and Henderson 1977; J. Beers 1974). Thus the alphabet approach did work, and later I will show why, in some measure, this was so.

The ABC method did not, however, *always* work. To return blindly to the "good old days" would be a grave mistake. Amusing evidence for this fact is given by Charles Hoole in his work titled, *A New Discovery of the Old Art of Teaching School*, written in 1759.

> This course we see hath been very effectual in a short time, with some more ripe witted children, but others of a slower apprehension (as the most and best most commonly are) have been thus learning a whole year together (and though they have been chid and beaten too for want of heed) could scarce tell six of letters at twelve month's end, who if they had been taught in a way more agreeable to their meane apprehensions (we might have wrought more readily upon their senses, and affected their minds with what they did) would doubtless have learned as cheerfully if not as fast as the quickest.

Hoole's eminent good sense about his art would serve us well today; for while we seldom beat children now to make them learn, we do often apply the fiercest psychological pressure. Hoole judged that he was wrong to have done this; and so, I think, are we.

The rote drill, tiresome memorization and recitation that characterized most primary reading instruction of this period stemmed, I believe, from two sources. The first was religious-cultural; the Puritan ethic demanded stern self-discipline of all, and of the young in particular. As such, this way of teaching may be thought to be a factor over and above methodology. Of course it is true that certain methods lend themselves more naturally to prescriptive drill than permissive reason. Nonetheless, cultural imperatives are, or should be, superficial to method as such.

The second source of the emphasis on drill was a psychological one. The outlook of the time was that young children had the capacity to remember and only later did they gain the capacity to reason. This circumstance is viewed very differently today; nonetheless, the earlier position was not an altogether silly one. This recognition that the cognitive processes of young children differ from those of older children is impressive, for it suggests an intuitive awareness of that developmental shift from pre-operational to concrete operational thought so brilliantly researched and described by Piaget (1967). Prior to age six and a half or seven, though with wide variation among normal children, young children do not manage data relationally. They can deal with length or width, volume or mass, but not length in relation to width or volume in relation to mass (Flavell 1963). Work by Zutell (1980) and C. Beers (1976) shows that this cognitive limitation does have important implications for the stages by which learning to read progresses.

☐ The McGuffey Reader

By the mid-1800s, as the population of our country grew, the dame school and the one-room schoolhouse began to give way to schools with graded classrooms. With this transition came the need for graded materials for reading instruction, of which perhaps the best known were the long-enduring *McGuffey Readers* (1866). These were and are a most interesting pedagogical production, though I would not, as others have done, recommend them as the solution to our educational needs today.

One major thrust of this series was to involve the young learners in reading material that was morally stimulating and inspiring. This was in keeping with Mr. McGuffey's principal vocation as a professor of theological philosophy—a chair he held at the University of Virginia for some forty years.

A more interesting aspect of the series, from a methodological point of view, was the manner by which grade levels were attained. Formulae were not used—either for sentence length or vocabulary choice. Words were not repeated for reinforcement. Such techniques were not to come into use until very much later. Rather it appears that the texts were composed intuitively on the basis of what was thought to be apprehensible by children of various ages. In modern parlance we might call this design an intuitive semantic or meaning control. It is an approach that would necessarily require adjustment to changing times and cultures, but it is one that I will argue later may have remarkable merit.

Absent also in the *McGuffey Readers* was a program of phonics—a fact often times not realized by the casual observer, for word lists along with phonetic transcriptions were included. These, however, were designed for a very different purpose. McGuffey aimed here at providing a source of standard pronunciation for children in our dialectically different regions. Thus it was held that chimney should be pronounced "chimney" not "chimbley," as it was spoken in a good many rural areas.

☐ Formal Methods, 1870–1900

Reading methodologies in the formal sense seem not to have emerged in any force until about the 1870s. It was then that both the phonics and the whole-word approaches were composed into published reading programs. These two competitive methods may be described simply. In the phonics approach the multiple sounds represented by letters were taught directly and usually in isolation. Children were then taught to "sound words out" by blending the sounds of the individual letters together. In this way it was held that children would most quickly gain independence in pronouncing words not previously read. So armed, it was believed they might then read and spell with greater assurance and accuracy.

In the whole-word approach the child's ability to learn a word as easily as a letter was capitalized on. It was argued that by this means the year of drill on letter sounds could be bypassed, and pupils could, from the beginning, participate in thoughtful, productive reading.

In reviewing these two methods at the turn of the century, E. B. Huey found assets and liabilities in each. He considered the prolonged phonics drill intellectually debilitating for six year olds and likely to discourage an enthusiasm for reading. On the other hand, where no word analysis was conducted, as in a pure whole word approach, it appeared that pupils were deficient in recognizing "new words" and in spelling. Here then, seventy-five years ago, were the arguments pro and con. It is important that teachers and parents know, as many do not, that this difference of opinion is not new and that it has received the thoughtful consideration of educators for fully 100 years. Neither of these two extremes was found then, nor will they be found now, to be a panacea for teaching all to read.

Huey, with some reservations, took the position that the combination approach was best. In this, children made a beginning by learning whole words, but their reading lessons were accompanied by related lessons in phonics and word blending. He looked with favor upon the sentence method devised by Miss Cooke (see Huey 1908) in which children did their earliest reading in the material that they dictated to the teacher. He judged, however, that this approach too would need to be accompanied by related lessons in word study.

With but one exception, the prototypes of every reading methodology practiced today were designed, published, and used extensively prior to 1900. There was the Chinese method in which children shouted out their responses in noisy chorus—a tactic used by Bereiter and Englemann (1966) with the underprivileged in the late 1960s. There were a variety of phonetic programs in which a marked or augmented alphabet was used to signal the variations in sound that letters might represent. These were essentially the same as some "new" programs such as "Words in Color" (Gattegno 1964) and "i t a" (Mazurkiewicz and Tanzer 1963). There were strict phonics programs, similar to the present-day Economy series (Harris *et al.* 1960), and there were combination programs that varied by shades and gradations in the emphasis placed on word study.

Huey marveled at the ingenuity and beauty of many of these materials. His principal criticism was of the inanity of the content of the primary materials and the narrow and excessive emphasis placed on skills and reading texts as opposed to experiences, books, and reading to some purpose. His admiration and his concerns are equally applicable to most of our contemporary reading programs.

☐ Behaviorism and Method, 1900–1950

Changes indeed have occurred in these prototype methodologies of the 1890s, the most marked of which can be traced to the influence of the new science of psychology. The period from 1900 to 1950 was a time of vast technological expansion. In one generation we accelerated from horse drawn runabouts to globe-girding jets, and our faith in scientific solutions to all problems was boundless. It was then quite natural that our concepts of education should have shifted from pedagogy as an art to teaching as a technological science. Not only did the findings of psychological research influence reading instruction, but also, and more subtly, the model or theory behind such research cast its spell over all education. This theory, termed radical empiricism or behaviorism, dominated the American psychological scene from the turn of the century well into the mid-1950s.

The behavioral psychologists spurned what they held to be idle and nonscientific speculation about the mind and limited themselves to the study of overt measurable events. The effect of this position on pedagogy was an ever more detailed focus on the manipulation, control, and measurement of the surface content and surface effects of instructional programs. The broader concerns about what children thought, believed and "knew" were largely neglected.

Between 1900 and 1950, the combination method, an early compromise between the whole word and phonics strategies, dominated the educational scene. It was this general plan that formed the foundation for most new reading programs. The construction of the materials themselves, however, became even more "scientific" and formalized. Studies of the frequency of word usage, such as those by Thorndike and Lorge (1944), led to the practice of introducing frequently used words first and controlling the rate and volume of word introduction. So firm a grasp did this logic take that early reading ability soon was looked on as synonymous with the memorization of such core vocabularies. The new standardized reading tests, which themselves required little more than the naming of such words, reinforced a word learning focus, while the circularity of this teaching-testing regimen seemed to go altogether unnoticed.

To insure that the basic sight vocabulary would be learned, abstract principles of behavioral learning theory were applied directly to the language design of the readers. Each new word was introduced and then repeated in the text according to a rough schedule of reinforcement. The effect that this practice had on the content and style of primary materials was predictable and led to the grotesque and widely burlesqued diction of "Dick and Jane," those well-known characters in the archetypal basal reader of the 1950s (Gray et al. 1956).

True to the basic combination method, authors of these programs were committed to early reading, to stories that said something and got somewhere, and to the teaching of comprehension as well as word-attack skills. But in due course, comprehension training too came under the behavioral mask.

The new standardized tests of reading comprehension consisted almost entirely of short passages followed by questions. In response to these measurement devices the teaching of reading comprehension soon became a routine of asking pupils questions after they had read each page or story in their reader. Despite the fact that many scholars of that day wrote about the "tyranny of the right answer" and the deleterious effects of this way of teaching (Smith and Hullfish 1961, for example), this questioning practice would become so established that many even now may wonder that I should challenge it. The problem is this: the *process* of comprehension, or understanding, is not the same thing as answering a question derived from such comprehension. As a consequence, the answer to a question, whether right or wrong, gives the learner no solid information at all about how he has acquired such knowledge.

Equally important, the use of routine recitation sets an arbitrary and inflexible standard for comprehension which disregards the reader's prior knowledge and intellectual purpose. This trend in reading instruction is a typical example of the influence of the behavioral science theory. Absolutely critical, covert mental actions are disregarded while emphasis is placed alone on a surface response.

Soon, the questions asked pupils after reading were analyzed into various types. It was supposed that there are questions of literal fact, general fact, inference, sequence, judgment, and the like. These, in turn, were relegated to different categories of "comprehension skills," and they were introduced and practiced by the student in a workbook which accompanied the reader and which was designed in the fashion of a behavioral reinforcement schedule. This practice continues today even though educational psychologists have failed repeatedly to demonstrate any real differences among these so-called comprehension skills (e.g., Davis 1944; Thurstone 1946; Hunt 1952; Lennon 1962; Thorndike 1973).

A still further facet of measurement, the readability formula, had its influence on the construction of basal readers and on most other school texts as well. Since sentence length and vocabulary frequency predicted performance on power tasks in reading (the McCall exercises, 1961, for example), it was judged that the difficulty of reading material could be manipulated by the length of the sentences and frequency of certain words. As a result, textbook authors have regularly constrained their writing to use of shorter sentences and high-frequency vocabularies. The obvious result was that the quality of style and integrity of content in these readers was further eroded.

Those who have lived through this period and have become accustomed to the simplified writings designed for beginning readers will doubtless wonder again at my challenging so well established an educational tool as the readability formula. It should be understood that it is not the formula that I object to, but rather its misuse. In fact, recent work by Jacobson (1974), in which he uses orthographic complexity as a prediction variable, shows unusual power and promise. One implication from this work, for example, is that word knowledge has dimensions other than those of simple frequency of occurrence. What does not follow from such work, however, is that material can or should be artificially constructed either by frequency or by complexity in order to meet decreasing levels of readability. We must remind ourselves that youth have learned to read using *Pilgrim's Progress*, the *Book of Common Prayer*, and the King James version of the *Bible* when those works were a significant aspect of their culture. Further, at the higher grades, we must distinguish between the legitimate or common sense practice of selecting readable books from the very questionable practice of contriving books so that they can be read.

☐ The 1950s Basal Reader

By 1950, the typical basal reader program was composed in this way. For grade one, there were two expendable readiness books, two or three paperback preprimers, a hardback primer, and a first grade reader, the latter two with accompanying workbooks. For the teacher a large manual duplicated the children's texts and contained explicit directions for administering each task.

For second and third grades, two readers and two workbooks were employed, and thereafter a single text and workbook were provided for grades four, five, and six. The rate of vocabulary introduction varied somewhat from series to series, but typically averaged about 400 words in grade one, about 500 words in grade two, and perhaps 600 or more in grade three. About eighty percent of these words fell into the "highest frequency" categories (Dzama 1972).

The usual reading lesson advanced as follows. First, the teacher wrote the "new" or "to-be-introduced" words on the blackboard, usually in simple sentences. Then she called on children to read them, helping as needed. When these new words had been learned, the story was introduced, as directed by the manual. Typically, this consisted of a discussion of the pictures and of the principle concepts that were to be dealt with in the reading. For example, "Today our little friends are going to a pet store. Can you name some of the pets they will see?" Next, the teacher would declare one or more purposes for the reading: "Read the first page and see which pet they want to buy."

Following this preparation or "readiness for reading," pupils were directed to read the page silently. This was then followed by questions designed to cover the content of the page. The original purpose question, "What pet will they buy?" might or might *not* be honored in this process. When a story had been completed, most teachers had their pupils reread the story aloud, calling on the students in order—the so-called round-robin oral reading method. (Manuals of the time deplored this practice, but, interestingly, teachers did it anyway!)

Word study or phonics was advanced in the workbook exercises and followed a well-established pattern. In the readiness and pre-primer materials, children were taught to turn pages and follow simple directions. They were taught how to use crayons and primary pencils and to place objects and pictures in a left-right progression. Practice was given in making basic auditory discriminations and in manual matching tasks with objects, letters, and words. In the preprimers, of course, the first twenty-five to fifty words were introduced: "Oh, oh, oh, see, see, see. Oh, see. Oh, see. Oh, see," and so on.

In grade two, the discrimination of letter blends was taught, i.e., *bl*ack and *bl*ue begin alike, wa*nt* and pla*nt* end alike, and then the short vowel patterns were introduced, i.e., c*o*t, n*e*t, s*i*t, t*o*p, c*u*p. Long vowel patterns, as with the silent *e* in h*o*me and the silent *a* in b*o*at, were usually reserved for grade three, where the three syllabication rules were taught as well. In grade four, the diphthongs were added, and use of the dictionary was taught. Such, briefly, was the pace of the typical basal reader "analytic phonics" program.

A survey conducted in the 1950s showed that a basal reader program of this general type was used in about ninety percent of the elementary classrooms in the United States (Austin and Morrison 1961). These methods, however, were not without their critics. In most independent schools and in communities where prescriptiveness and academic "rigor" were cherished, intensive, usually synthetic, phonics programs were most often used. Elsewhere, more naturalistic approaches were preferred. These latter usually followed a variation of Miss Cooke's sentence method (see Huey 1908), and a wide variety of children's books were used instead of a basal reader.

☐ Sputnik and the Linguistic Influence

In the early 1950s, a fire of phonics enthusiasm was ignited by Rudolph Flesch with his best-seller, *Why Johnny Can't Read* (Flesch 1955). Immediately, however, a stalwart army of reading experts beat back the blaze. Basal readers continued triumphant until the Russians launched the first satellite into space. With Sputnik overhead, an outraged and badly frightened public turned on an educational system that they thought had failed them. Books like *What Ivan Knows That Johnny Doesn't* (Trace 1961) showed, for example, that the rate of vocabulary introduction in the Russian readers boldly exceeded that in ours—1,000 words in grade one instead of 400.

Across the land, substantive scientists, psychologists, and linguists were enlisted to correct the faulty system (Bruner 1960). From these experts, new approaches to the teaching of science and mathematics soon emerged. To the rescue of reading, however, came the ideas of the linguist Bloomfield (1933) and the operant conditioning strategies of B. F. Skinner (1957), both of whom were behaviorists. That things happened in this way is curious and a little ironic, for a great deal of the reform of this time reflected the ideas of a new breed of psychologists who were moving rapidly away from the rigidity and surface-limited concepts of behaviorism. Bruner, for example, was concerned that pupils not simply memorize the facts of science but that they learn to think as a scientist, that they become not simply problem solvers but problem finders as well. For reading, however, this was not so. Instead, we adopted programs of super-behavioristic form and theories from an age that was past.

Bloomfield's ideas about reading were formulated in the 1930s and were advanced to prominence in the early 1960s (nearly ten years after his death) by a second distinguished linguist, Charles Fries (1962). Both men were language scientists who approached their work under the theoretical model of behaviorism. It appears that Bloomfield's interest in reading came about almost by accident when he found that his son was having difficulty in learning to read in first grade. From his perspective, the programs of instruction being used did violence to the scientific facts about English orthography, and, resourcefully, he set out to write a plan that would comport with these truths.

A central tenet for the behavioral linguist was that spoken language is the primary data base for the study of language. Written language was viewed as a code bonded to the elements of speech by direct associative links. Both Bloomfield and Fries held that thinking had nothing whatsoever to do with reading, an idea which at that time struck me as patently false. That I have changed my opinion about there being a dichotomy between language and thought should not in any way suggest, however, that I have returned to a Bloomfieldian view of language. His focus was on the language surface—as a puzzle to be analyzed and taught in pieces by conditioning. Ours is a focus on the child as a cognitively endowed language learner.

It seemed logical to Bloomfield that pupils should first learn the letters of the alphabet and next the linguistically regular patterns. He recommended that they name each letter of the pattern and then say it naturally and as a whole: "C-A-T, Cat," "R-A-T, Rat," and so on. Because phonemes exist only in the context of the full spoken syllable, he was opposed to the attempts made in phonics programs to teach isolated letter sounds or to sound out words on a letter-by-letter basis. He judged that when the regular forms could be identified automatically, then irregular words would be more readily noticed and remembered.

There is in Bloomfield's plan a sweetness of logic and simplicity, as well as a powerful informedness about phonology, that is most appealing. Moreover, much that he advocated is simply and straightforwardly correct (as has been substantiated through work at the Haskins Laboratory, see Liberman 1973). To implement Bloomfield's program, however, one must envision an early primary experience reminiscent of that of the alphabet approach. Not all children learned their letters then nor is there any reason to expect them to do so today. The claims of infallibility for this program on the basis of "scientific proof" are not well founded.

If one follows Bloomfield's plan, one must acquiesce to a situation in which young children spend a year or more reciting nonsense—e.g., "Can a pan fan a man?" This occurs because the application of the strict control for letter-sound regularity decimates any English sentence. Clearly, there are pieces missing from the puzzle in the Bloomfield proposal, and it is precisely these pieces—meaning and the mind—that the behavioral scientist purposely fails to consider.

Only one program today follows Bloomfield's approach with reasonable fidelity (Bloomfield and Barnhart 1963), but most show his influence. In nearly every reading series now, linguistic terms are used. Word-attack for example is called decoding. Letter-sound relationships are called phoneme-grapheme relationships. Such are simply the trimmings of "popular science." In addition, regularly occurring spelling patterns are more widely used, and these patterns are selected and explained more accurately than was done in earlier phonics programs. Thus a terminology change and an improved phonological theory have been applied to the 100-year-old combination basal and synthetic phonics. These adaptations, however, are quite alien to the plan that Bloomfield himself advocated.

In addition, the basal readers today use a new system of word introduction. When a word pattern has been taught, it is deemed that other words of the same class are now "decodable" and thus may be included. For example, when the silent *i* or *i* marker, in the pattern *rain*, has been presented, this allows the use of *main, Spain,* and *plain* in the plan of vocabulary control. By this means, vocabulary loads have been substantially increased; we have caught up to Ivan, and the quality and style of writing has been somewhat improved.

Two further changes have occurred, one partly in response to a very influential monograph by Jeanne Chall, *Learning to Read: The Great Debate* (1967), the other a result of the cultural revolution of the 1960s. After reviewing a large number of methodological comparison studies, Chall drew the conclusion that success, particularly in grade one, seemed to fall to those programs in which more intensive and more rapidly paced phonics or word-study activities were applied. Accordingly, she declared that reading programs should feature a decoding emphasis. The new basals have complied. Vowel patterns that heretofore were taught in grade three are now taught in grade one, and the full array of decoding skills is panoramically displayed in minutely detailed charts of scope and sequence. In addition, the stereotypic stories of the 1950s have been largely rooted out. There are now stories of great variety, most of them more beautifully illustrated than ever, and minorities mingle freely in an egalitarian world. Beneath this surface, however, the formulae of construction remain in command, and these are still contrived and unnatural works.

☐ **Programmed Reading and Accountability**

Concurrently with the Bloomfieldian influence came that of the program writers whose work derived from the theoretical ideas of B. F. Skinner. As we have seen, behavioral science had long influenced the general plan of the basal reader. Vocabulary, comprehension skills, and word-attack skills were all laid out in a rough schedule of reinforcement. Now, however, a new systematization was employed that undertook to identify, order, and reinforce each molecular skill that was guessed to comprise the reading act. Sullivan's *Programmed Reading* (Buchanan 1963) is the clearest example of this trend.

One glaring misconception in all such programs is the assumption that we know, at an elementary level, what the skills of the reading process are or that we know the order by which these skills are mastered. In fact we do not, and so, for all their appearance of rigor and tidiness, preparation of these materials is wholly intuitive. Our more global studies of childrens' developmental knowledge of word will show that these programs of skills are often grossly incomplete and very often faulty in the ordering decreed.

In an age of accountability, the format of these systems has been widely adapted to the standard basal programs through the writing of behavioral objectives and the use of sequence charts and checklists of skills, e.g., the Wisconsin Design (Otto and Askov 1970). What earlier was treated fairly broadly as knowledge of beginning consonants has here been partitioned into listing the individual initial consonants, along with a planned activity and mastery test for each. One somewhat alarming effect of this manic effort to account for things has been that the time spent in testing and accounting has consumed a greater and greater proportion of the teaching day. Put differently, the isolated skills of reading have tended to displace reading itself (Morris 1979; Allington 1980). One reaction to this circumstance may be seen in the popular fad of scheduling a half-hour period each day to be used for "uninterrupted silent reading" by every person in a school. Worthy as the idea is, it bespeaks a certain academic desperation!

Spelling Instruction

While there are important differences between spelling and reading instruction, there are also equally important commonalities. From at least the fifteenth century on, throughout our colonial period and in the early days of the new United States, the teaching of spelling and the teaching of reading were a single enterprise. Noah Webster's "Blue-Backed Speller" was the primary reading program of that era.

It was not until graded classrooms were formed and separate readers produced that spelling and reading began to split apart. By the 1870s, as we have seen, reading instruction began to be influenced by methodologists who constructed nicely reasoned but quite divergent plans for primary teaching. This was the beginning of the reading-method wars that have continued to the present day.

Curiously, there were no comparable methodological prescriptions offered for the teaching of spelling. It is true, of course, that reading instruction was thought to influence spelling. Huey (1908), for example, was of the opinion that the alphabet method might have had some positive effects on spelling. He also seemed to believe that an analysis of word structure, as part of the "Combination Method," would do the same. But nowhere in the last century do we find for spelling any highly visible method that would guarantee success.

This is not to imply, however, that correct spelling was not prized. It has been said, and I am inclined to agree, that there were but three academic levels in our society—those who had been to college, those who spelled correctly, and those who were semiliterate. The spelling bee was not an idle game to heighten motivation; it was serious business. And for every ten wearers of a dunce cap it is likely that eight at least spelled *separate* with three *e's*.

Why then were there no methods? Well, of course there were, after a fashion—the method was to memorize. Variations of this "method" included memorize words, memorize syllables, memorize rules, memorize high frequency words. (Here we see the influence of the psychological studies of the 1920s.) Thence came memorize words by a schedule of reinforcement and so all the possible strategies of association and over-learning derived from behavioral science were applied. Many put considerable store in "visualizing words to be remembered." Pupils were told to close their eyes and "see" the word. There was not much said, however, about how this could actually come about.

For all of this effort there were few experts who dared claim that their method was infallible, as was and still is done for methods of teaching reading. Evidence to the contrary was always too clearly at hand. Unlike reading, spelling exacts an unrelenting and absolutely visible criterion of success. Even a very weak reader may hold up a book or newspaper and seem to get forward with it. He may also plead lack of time and a host of other pressing interests and responsibilities. But for the speller, pen in hand, the die is cast. His sin will soon be there for all to see.

Is then spelling like reading, or is it quite different? Absolute non-readers can't spell, but there are many reasonably able readers who spell very poorly (Frith 1980). Spelling in this sense seems to be more demanding than reading. The criterion for success in reading, however, is less rigorous; much sloppy workmanship can pass unnoticed. Further, for spelling, while the error is clearly visible, what underlies the error is most obscure. It may then be that the differences in difficulty between reading and spelling are more apparent than real.

The studies we have made of children's errors in spelling have led us to infer that important conceptual ideas do indeed underlie what letters a child will select to represent a word. In addition we have come to believe that these conceptual stages have significance both for learning to read and for learning to spell. Not surprisingly, then, our tendency pedagogically is toward a recombining of the spelling and reading curriculum, particularly in the primary years. It is encouraging to find that we are not alone in this conviction (C. Chomsky 1971).

A look at the history of the English language and the way that it has come to be spelled will be helpful at this point. The topic, of course, is a large one, and only the barest outline can be conveyed here; but it will go a long way toward showing why spelling has been treated as it has in our educational system.

☐ An Historical Perspective

To begin at the beginning, we may think of England as being inhabited by the ancient Briton—a Celtic speaker, only moderately literate. It was to these shores that Caesar came at last and met a resistance more formidable than he expected. He fared better on a second attempt but bore no tribute home beyond a promissory note which remained uncollected (Baugh 1957).

In due course, however, England was colonized by the Romans. There were cities (London among them) and camps; there were roads and villas. One can see today, excavated beneath the foundations of Yorkminster, parts of a Roman camp, its plan and painted walls. Then, after nearly 400 years, the Romans departed abruptly. Teutonic tribes, the Angles, Saxons, and Jutes, swept in from the low countries of Europe driving the remaining Celts before them to the west and the north. Almost nothing of the language or culture from the preceding period has remained. The English language thus had its beginning in the gradual amalgamation of dialects of these Germanic invaders.

A very high level of literacy was attained during the Saxon period, contrary to my earlier ill-informed notions. Christianization began about the year 600 and with it came the founding of monasteries and the production of books. These were written at first in Latin, and Northumbria is said to have become at this time a European center for learning and scholarly production. By the close of the seventh century, Old English began also to be written. There followed a period of recession when the Vikings swept over much of Europe and actually settled in eastern England. By the end of the tenth century, however, the nation was reunited under Saxon rule, and monasteries were reformed under the Benedictine order. English became then the principal language (an unparalleled use of the vernacular in Europe at that period), and the production of books resumed its former vigor.

Scragg (1974) describes in detail the remarkable degree of uniformity then attained in the spelling system and shows how this persisted for over a century. With his help one may read a rendition of "The Lord's Prayer" attributed to Abbot Aelfric, ca. 990, and like him you will marvel at the "majestic simplicity of this prose" (Scragg 1974, p. 9).

Scragg shows that this spelling system was far more regular in phoneme-grapheme correspondence than is modern English. Nonetheless, there were spelling "curiosities" that have continued: the voiced and voiceless *th*, represented by /ð/ or /θ/, indiscriminately; the letter *s* used for both /s/ and /z/; the ambivalent use of *y* for *i* for a common vowel. It seems most clear, however, that it was this early and unusual stabilization of written English that has underpinned the historical, as opposed to the phonetic, ordering of contemporary spelling.

While we may still read Abbot Aelfric's prayer, Old English then was very different from English now, and the story of its evolution is remarkable. Old English was heavily inflected, like Latin and Greek; specific endings to nouns, adjectives, and verbs indicated syntactic relationships. These were gradually eroded, and English changed to its present analytic form in which word order in a sentence governs the "who did what to whom" of meaning. In addition, successive invasions, both martial and civil, have brought in great stocks of vocabulary borrowings—Danish, early Latin, early French, classical Latin and Greek, late French, Dutch and Spanish, and from the colonies bits and pieces from the world around. From this embarrassment of riches, English dropped the habit of forming new words from the native stock as German does, e.g., instead of "*naturesearcher*" (*naturwissenschaft*), English came to use a borrowing (from Greek) like "*scientist.*"

The erosion of inflections began as the various Saxon dialects were conjoined. The rapidity of this erosion increased when Danish gradually was absorbed into the language over a period of several hundred years (850–1050 A.D.). We owe a goodly number of basic words and spelling forms to the Vikings. The *sk* of *sky* and *skin* and *scrub* are Scandinavian, while the *sc* of Old English has been changed in sound to *sh* as in *ship* and *shall*. Something of the "coziness" and the egalitarian quality of this blending may be seen in our pair words *shirt* and *skirt* from Old English *scyrte* and Old Norse *skyrta* (Baugh 1957, p. 113).

The Norman invasion of 1066 was very different from that of the Danes, for while all of England was conquered, only the ruling class was replaced by speakers of Norman French. England became, as a consequence, a truly bilingual nation, but one that was divided sharply at the line of literacy.

The literary tradition of the Saxon scribes gradually failed. Norman French became the language of the court, law, and religion. Unimpeded by the settling influence of writing, spoken English thence continued in its course of change. Such writing as did occur in English shows a clear differentiation into dialectical areas and a breakdown of the old spelling standard. There were, however, high points of interest—the Wycliffe Bible and the influence of the Collards and a manuscript by Orm in which a remarkably modern spelling system was evolved to mark the altered language. Chaucer's works were the crowning achievement of the late period.

It was to be the language of London, however, upon which modern English would be formed. By the close of the fourteenth century, England had become a nation wholly separate from France—civilly, psychologically, and in language. Following the black plague in 1347, there occurred a great rise in the merchant class, the hub of which was London. By 1430, the language of court, law, and trade was English and to this broader, more secular demand came cheaper paper and the printing press.

From 1066 to 1430, the evolution of modern English was rapidly completed. Phonological changes affecting the discriminant vowels and consonants went forward continuously. Inflectional endings gradually disappeared, and their role was supplanted by the ordering of words in sentences and text. In addition, a large borrowing from the Anglo-Norman vocaculary was made—on the order of about forty percent of our present vocabulary.

The period of Middle English seems rather like a great pot of 100-year soup on the back burner of a rural stove. The ancient stock persisted, and it combined and blended in interesting and agreeable ways, while the weekly lacing of French wine continually added piquancy, a certain elegance, and new power. The basic stuff was English, the high frequency words and function words of the grammar. To these, French terms of court, law, religion, and war were added.

Not surprisingly, spelling too was influenced by this pottage of changing sounds and conventions. Some changes were very convenient, some were perplexing and continue to be so. As we have seen, English spelling had long strayed from that consistency of form established in the tenth century. Sound patterns too had changed so that the spelling of Middle English became increasingly abstract. By the fifteenth century, the diphthong *ea* of Old English, for example, had collapsed with our present short *e*. In French, the same diphthong had changed, but somewhat differently. These shifts and borrowings yield us today the troublesome variable in words like *each*, *break*, and *bread*. The unsounded *h* of late classical Latin and French has given us the bothersome *h* of *honor*, *herb*, and *horrible*; yet as a marker, *h* has served well to make the old *sc* of "scippe" in *ship* and the *c* of "cynn" in *chin* less ambiguous. Also the plagued final /s/, heretofore conveniently spelled *s*, arrived in its spelling of *ce* in French borrowings like *dance* and *fence* and *chance*.

The next two centuries were to see a continuing change, but there would also be a formalization of that change wrought by printers. Lexicographers would follow much later and legitimize these changes for the general public.

Publication and sale of books, then as now, was governed by the marketplace, and the early printers of English were in fact men of business. They settled on the language of the consumer, the mercantile, and governing class centered in London. Spelling was adopted to the type faces available and shaped to an even greater consistency. Where borrowings continued, as they did in great measure from classical Latin and Greek, the logic of derivational consistency was employed, albeit not always correctly. The final *z* in *prize*, deriving as it does from the past tense of *prendre-pris*, should doubtless be spelled with an *s* as it is in *surprise*, yet it serves as a distinction from *prise* meaning *lever*. The curious *s* in *island* also is "wrong." It was thought to have been derived from *insula*, but that is not so. The Old English word was *ieg* requiring no *s* at all. But rightly, as most of these printers were, or wrongly, as now and then occurred, there was nonetheless a logic to the consistency that was reached. Conspicuously, however, it was not a logic built upon letter-sound correspondence.

Middle English at its prime brought us the works of Chaucer; modern English at its beginning gave us the writings of Shakespeare—literary achievements unsurpassed in any human language. By the achievements of those two men of literary genius, the power of the English language is validated beyond any critical quarrel. Chaucer, however, is removed from the modern reader both by sound and vocabulary. In the intervening time, English "long" vowels completed a change that would separate them from both Middle English and other European languages. Formerly the letter *i* was pronounced /i/ as in *meet*. It became the diphthong /ay/ as in *fine*. The letter *a* was pronounced /ɑ/ as in *hard*. It became the diphthong /ei/ as in *same*. The short vowels did not change. Spelling, however, was already largely fixed to the earlier, originally quite phonetic, representation. Thus *make*, pronounced by Chaucer with two syllables /m/ /k/, is pronounced /meik/ and spelled *make*, with its vestigial inflection *e* unpronounced but "useful" as a mark of a long vowel.

The Great Vowel Shift of English is of considerable interest to the present work because we have found that the old phonological relationship between the spelling of long and short vowels seems intuitively to be preferred by young children when they begin to write. It accounts for a consistent and conspicuous incidence of "error" in their early attempts to spell modern English. Their preference works backward through the change of circumstance. Finding that the sound /i/ is attached to, is the name of, the letter *e*, they assume that the sound /I/ as in pin should also be represented with the letter *e*. Accordingly, they spell the word *sit*, SET; the word *fish*, FES; and so on (Read 1970).

The vocabulary change between Chaucer's works and Shakespeare's was a consequence of the Renaissance—a rediscovery of that culture whose citizens had departed English shores a thousand years before. To the already abundant borrowing of ecclesiastical Latin from earliest times and of Anglo-Norman in the Middle period came then our vast classical vocabulary of philosophy, science, and art. It was this composite language that gradually stabilized to its present spoken and written form. Sound changes have continued, though more slowly than before. Spelling has changed also but not drastically. Unlike Chaucer, Shakespeare may be read directly from a distance of 400 years.

It was not until the eighteenth century that a proper dictionary of modern English appeared. The first was compiled by Bailey in 1721, the most famous and most influential by Johnson in 1755. Scragg (1974, p. 81) observes that the power of Johnson's work lies primarily in the elegance and force of his writing rather than in any particular lexographical contribution. In terms of spelling, Johnson accepted the conventional, i.e., the printers' standard, and by so doing projected this standard to the private sector. For centuries, considerable variability in spelling had been accepted among the laity, if not in printed documents. However, by the close of the eighteenth century, correct spelling by a single standard was expected of all literate Englishmen.

In America, where informal writing became even more idiosyncratic than in England, a comparably influential standard for private writing was not set until the publication of Noah Webster's *An American Dictionary of the English Language* in 1824. In this work a number of spelling innovations were advanced which have persisted—most noticeable among these are *music* and *public* without a final *k*, *honor* and *color* without a *u*, and *center* spelled *er* rather than *re*. By and large, however, this work was as conservative as Johnson's and as influential in establishing the doctrine of correctness.

I sometimes reflect wryly that my grandfather, born in 1824, grew up in an age of liberal private spelling, while his daughter and I, bad spellers both, have had to struggle under Mr. Webster's standard. Such self-pity, however, is not warranted. While variations were long permitted, gross inconsistencies never were, and they, not error, are the mark of the deficient speller. Still, it seems worth pointing out that an absolute standard is a relatively new event. It is also one that has tended to blind us to the value of accepting those normal and consistent errors that children all make as they gradually learn our complex spelling system.

And it should be recognized that the printers' standard for spelling is complex. Englishmen, particularly English school teachers, have been vigorously and vocally aware of this fact for centuries. In the mid-1500s, serious proposals were written to simplify and regularize English spelling in relation to sound (Hart 1569, Bollokar 1581, for example. See Scragg 1974). But, the contrary view was also argued then—that while English spelling should be consistent, it need not serve sound only; it worked quite well for the literate, and learning a new form would be a nuisance (Mulcaster 1582. See Scragg 1974).

When Samuel Johnson put his stamp of approval upon the printers' standard, he did so deliberately. He was concerned that written English maintain its readability against the inevitable sound changes of a living language. He approved of consistency and derivational purity (though he often broke the rule and usually deferred to custom). He also was wary of modern borrowings and feared that if translations were not discouraged we would soon all be babbling like Frenchmen

(McAdam and Milne 1963). A very human man, conservative and proud of his country, vastly learned and articulate, Johnson carried the argument for his day.

The desire for a simpler spelling system nonetheless rose again. Noah Webster began as a conservative; his "Blue-Backed Speller" echoed the Johnson line. He then became a radical reformer, only to reform himself again recommending only modest changes in his dictionary. Benjamin Franklin, whose scholarship Webster had the effrontery to derogate (Vallins 1973), invented a simplified spelling plan, though he did not seriously press its acceptance.

For the remainder of the nineteenth century, spelling reformers became increasingly active, some might even say strident, in their pleas: English spelling was too difficult for children and foreigners to learn. The pain of failure and time wasted in the teaching of it were deplorable. Yet the public remained curmudgeonly indifferent, resisting the most ingenious and gentle proposals for reform as easily as those more antic and bizarre.

To Henry Bradley (1918) must go the laurel for the twentieth-century's defense of bad, old, conservative, and difficult-to-learn English. He argued that the purpose of written language is not to represent sound but meaning, and to do so as efficiently and as unambiguously as possible. He saw in the homonym and stable root (*Canada, Canadian; critic, criticize,* for example), an ideographic quality suited to the speaker of English be he learned or merely literate. In his view modern English spelling approaches an optimum of efficiency that would be decimated by a simple phonetic rendering.

Once again the enthusiasm of the language reformers had been quashed. But the serpent of discontent will rise again unless the evils of learning to spell are met and mastered. The thesis of this present work is that standard English can be taught practically, efficiently, and painlessly to all normal language users. In taking this position I reject the need for drastic reform and challenge the posture of the conservatives as well who argue that our spelling system is good for readers but for spellers terribly bad.

It was not until the early sixties that I found the opportunity to read Albert Baugh's fine work *The History of the English Language.* In this, however, he treated spelling somewhat at arm's length. He declared it *bad* for the learner and noted that there was, at that time, no adequate history of its evolution. This void has now been ably filled by the works of Vallins (1973) and Scragg (1974), but they too seem convinced that English spelling must be very hard to learn.

I agree fully with Scragg that educators, and perhaps psycholinguists as well, have been derelict in their neglect of language history. That Bradley's masterful argument (1918) against spelling reform is so little known is an egregious example of this neglect. Even so, the general pessimism of these scholars has lent but little support to pupils and teachers.

Admittedly, English spelling is complex, but so are children. Our studies show some of the wonderfully complex adjustments that even very young children make to the spelling system as they find it. History shows an evolutionary order in the form of written English, and it is this order, perhaps not surprisingly, that children follow as they gradually assimilate the conventions of English spelling. Educators need simply to aid children in this progress rather than oppose them with rules and exceptions based on a false assumption that words should be spelled as they sound.

□ Current Research in Spelling

What else was done about spelling instruction in the 1920s? Cahen's review of research in 1971 tells the story adequately. Beginning in the 1960s, some interesting investigations of phonemic regularity in English were taking place, and the Chomskian view was emerging. These then current ideas will be discussed in Chapter 3 as the background for our studies presented here.

There were in the 1920s a large number of descriptive studies in which accountings were made of errors that occur in children's spelling. This work was quite like those in language acquisition research of the same period. What happened when children made spelling errors was carefully recorded, but no sense could be made of it. One of the most interesting studies in this group was that of Arthur Gates (1936) whose design elicited invented spellings by his subjects in grades two through eight. Many years later I heard Gates say to Hobart Mowrer that what he learned from the effort was that he didn't understand a thing about spelling. Today we can make some sense of his carefully executed research (Temple 1978). Along with descriptive studies of spelling errors and language acquisition research is a third area of study involving comparisons between one method of teaching and another. This work unfortunately is marred by its design, and no such study would be undertaken by any serious scholar today. That this same general comparison design continues to be encouraged by state and federal laws of accountability, however, is regrettable. That such studies are also used by authors and publishers as support for their programs is equally regrettable and misleading. I hope and expect that we will see less of such work in the future.

In 1980, two important reports of spelling research were published (Frith 1980; Kavanagh and Venezky 1980). They represent a wholly new thrust in this area after a lapse of nearly 100 years. To review this work is beyond our present scope, but to mention it with enthusiasm is gladly done. It might also be acceptable to report that a monograph of our own work joined this excellent company in the same year (Henderson and Beers 1980).

☐ A Personal Perspective, 1968

The search for a more adequate understanding of written English, soon to be vastly expanded by the application of cognitive psychological theory, is the substantive source from which our studies of children's word knowledge grew. In order to complete this perspective on reading and spelling instruction, I would like now to give a summary of my own views about reading as they stood a decade ago. Because I was fortunate in the teachers who came my way, I knew a good deal. As will appear, however, I did not know enough.

The Beginning. Those who learn to read and spell almost effortlessly are inclined to suppose that they achieve this happy state as a result of good minds, personal diligence, and a sound program of instruction. Those who do not are inclined to suspect a deficiency in all of these categories; moreover, if they do not, society is quick to suggest it. It has been my lot to be a member of the second group, and therewith began a life-long and very personal curiosity about how others learned to read and spell so easily.

In college I gained some power as a reader, which I attribute largely to the focus placed by my professors on thinking rather than on recitation. They followed, in essence, a Socratic approach, and I flourished under it. But my prowess in spelling resisted all efforts toward correction. I entered the teaching profession with at least the secondary hope that I might learn how to do somewhat better than was done for me.

In due course I turned to the reading field as a specialty and determined to enter the program offered at the University of Delaware, which was directed by a man whom I had seen teach a reading lesson to a group of third graders. I was fascinated by his technique. He asked the children what they *thought*. He goaded them to read with a purpose and to support their beliefs with evidence. It reminded me of my college days, and I believed that it was good. This fine teacher was Russell G. Stauffer. I came to study with him for a year and remained for ten as student and later, colleague.

A Different View of Reading in the 60s. Stauffer's ideas about reading were indeed Socratic, but they stemmed more directly from E. B. Huey (1908), Ernest Horn (1937), and John Dewey (1933). He tended to reject much of the influence of the behaviorists and to build instead upon the ideas of the semanticists of that period—Ogden and Richards (1946), for example. He argued that the essence of reading involved a communicative purpose, that it was an active process of reconstructing meaning, and that meaning kindled words, not words meaning.

This perspective was at sharp variance with the general plan for reading instruction that was common at that period. As described earlier, the combination readers advanced, as it were, word by word and in language that was structured by strict vocabulary control. The approach to comprehension was to ask questions of the pupil after he had read each passage. Stauffer's belief in the centrality of purpose and meaning made him insist that discussion should precede reading in order to elicit pupil purpose and that the lesson should close with evidence adduced by the child in support or denial of this commitment. Similarly, he held that new words should not be taught mechanically before the reading lesson but that they should be met in the act of reading, and only later reviewed and analyzed. While he advocated the use of basal readers with this altered procedure, he argued that a variation of the Cooke method (see Huey 1908)—now called the Language-Experience Approach—was best for beginners. For those who had begun to read he insisted that a major emphasis be placed on creative writing and that direct instruction be given in the reading of individually selected books having varied content and a minimum of artificial control.

The First Grade Studies. In the early 1960s, Stauffer participated in the well-known "first grade studies" (see Stauffer 1970). It is now generally agreed that these were meaningless enterprises as research. But as pedagogical adventures, I have always felt they were excellent and eminently worthwhile. Stauffer devoted himself fully to implementing a pure language-experience approach in a selected school district. His efforts were remarkably successful, and he had the extra good fortune to be able to follow these classes for a full six years. Comparisons of his sample group with a "control group" were favorable; the same can be said of most other similar efforts, using a wide range of very different methods. The importance of these kinds of studies is in the opportunity they provide skilled educators to commit themselves to their ideas about teaching and to follow them directly in the field. Such efforts yield far more than simple testimonials though these are not, I think, without their value too. One learns also what children do as they learn. Let me give an example.

In the first year of Stauffer's study, of which I was an observer, I think no one on the experimental staff had any idea of the beginning reader's ability to write creative stories in his own way and for himself. It had been planned that these students would be helped to make sentences using words they had learned which were printed on little chips of tag board. But early in the study, some children, frustrated at not finding a word that they wanted to use, took an empty chip and invented the word that they wanted. Had the teacher been under the clamp of some rigid manual this deviation would doubtless have been stopped. Stauffer and his team performed differently. They gave the children pencils and paper and urgedthem to write on their own. The results were fascinating. Of course wrong spellings abounded, but the content was delightful, and the errors were interestingly wrong.

Dorsey Hammond and I analyzed informally a sample of fifteen first graders' stories written in November. Fifty-one percent of the words were spelled correctly. In addition, another thirty percent of the errors seemed logical; for example, one child spelled *built*, BILLT. At a later time, Hammond followed the evolution of the word *elephant*

33

through one year's writing by one child. It began LFT, became ALAFAT, evolved to ELEFANT, and ended in all beauty as *elephant*. Clearly in this example there was no "negative conditioning from the learning of a wrong response"—that widely held, but spurious interpretation of learning theory for education. Instead there was an obvious and progressive mastery of orthographic convention.

The first-grade studies offered opportunities such as these. Far more important than being able to prove one method better than another, the educator-researcher in this situation was able to discover new questions, educational questions, to which substantive science might be able to speak. For my part, as an observer of Stauffer's work, I was profoundly moved to wonder what it was that children know about words and their spellings as they begin to learn to read.

Some Notions about Teaching Reading, 1969. Where, then, did I stand on the issue of reading ten years ago? First of all, I was fully persuaded that Stauffer's basic position was a sound one—that reading was a complex global human act and that learning to do so must take place in that context. I believed that the theories of the behaviorists and their influence, which led to the search for and the putative discovery of discrete skills of word knowledge and comprehension, was misguided. It therefore seemed to me that any synthetic program, be it by letter or sound or word at a time, would be found to do violence to the more global process that was to be learned. It also had begun to occur to me that the analytic programs—generally those of the great combination basal reader series—were also on shaky ground, for even though study activities might be set up on a more cognitive, thought-inducing, "discovery" basis, the thing to be discovered, "the skill," had an altogether uncertain validity.

Pedagogically my inclination was to move toward the most natural methods that I could bring myself to use. For beginning readers the language-experience approach seemed to me the best. It included a circumstance in which children were immersed in written language by being read aloud to from the widest possible array of story books. Thereafter, teacher-directed activities—simple everyday experiences like making butter, running down a hill, collecting leaves or seashells, a fire drill—were used as a basis for dictation by the children. These dictated stories or accounts were then read and reread for three or four days. Finally, words that the children knew were harvested and retained on cards in individual collections called word banks. There was a sharp difference between this sight vocabulary store and that designed for a basal reader series. No word frequency control was imposed, and no effort was made mechanically to "teach" these words. The bank was limited to those words that the children had come to know "naturally" in the course of reading their stories.

When children had attained a sight vocabulary of 200–300 words and were able to read with reasonable fluency some of their favorite story books, they were placed by groups in a basal reader and there directed in their reading after the Stauffer plan (see above). Opportunity for independent or free reading was scheduled on a regular basis. My decision to use the basal reader at all was frankly a compromise. I would have preferred a contemporary anthology written for children of first grade age but without any formal vocabulary or syntactic controls. The newer basal readers available at this time went a step in this direction and seemed at least acceptable.

Regarding word study and spelling, my thinking at this time was less advanced, and in retrospect, less consistent. What did children learn as they learned words? I simply did not know, nor did I have a theory about it. I did not think that children progressed linearly from isolated sounds to words. I supposed that what they learned was in part, at least, conceptual—the internalization of certain rules or pattern regularities after the Bloomfield (1933) idea. But what of the vast numbers of irregularities?

Given my state of ignorance, I reasoned that the conservative course would be to rely on the general outline or progression of word-study activities that had evolved in the basal programs over the past 100 years. I therefore advocated that auditory discrimination tasks be initiated early and intensively and that as soon as a small sight vocabulary had been attained, children should be taught to appreciate the sound-letter relationship for beginning consonants, then blends, ending consonants and blends, and from there to the short vowel patterns. I felt that this study should be conducted in the context of "known" words but that as mastery was attained, children should be helped to apply these understandings to unknown words in their directed reading lessons. Directed instruction was given for common prefixes, suffixes, and inflectional endings, the common long vowel pattern, rules for syllabication, and so on. In short, what I recommended in this area ten years ago, except for a more intensive pace, was very little different from that to which I had been exposed and helped to write in the Stauffer basal of the 1950s.

For spelling instruction, I followed a frankly behavioral approach. It seemed to me that the 5,000 most frequently occurring words should be checked on and memorized if necessary. I believed in adopting a spelling program and teaching it by planned stages of reinforcement. I hoped, indeed I expected, that the word analysis skills would not conflict with those taught in reading, and my tendency was to combine the two efforts.

The missing links in this teaching plan are now quite obvious. I did not know what English words afford the mind, and I did not know how children tackle these data. That much information *was* available to learners and that they, at least some of them, did act upon it, I strongly suspected. In the meantime I set children to those tasks that tradition recommended and hedged that bet with plans to reinforce recall. My one advantage was that I had a reasonably strong sense that I didn't know what I was talking about. It is an uncomfortable state of affairs but a good one for those who wish to learn.

Background and Beginnings   3

The Cognitive Revolution

☐ The Beginnings

The cognitive revolution came with a remarkable abruptness, but its roots were pressing outward from the close of World War II. Clark Hull's attempt (Hull *et al.* 1940) to extend the principles of behaviorism to mathematical form was clearly failing, and the once crystalline concepts of stimulus and response had begun their march toward becoming ever more abstract, covert, and essentially unmeasurable entities. From my very incomplete perspective at that time, the first major monograph I considered was that of Guilford. Splitting with the long-enduring single factor theory of intelligence (MacNemar 1964), he advanced, through a factor-analysis model, a multifaceted cognitive array of mental abilities. His ideas were presented in a presidential address to the American Psychological Association and appeared in the *American Psychologist* in December 1959 under the title "Three Faces of Intellect." I recall thinking then how well this design described many of the dimensions that we sought to exercise in Stauffer's plan for teaching reading comprehension. Divergent thinking—the ability to see multiple possibilities as opposed to finding right answers only—was a major emphasis of Stauffer's method. It was comforting to learn that an eminent psychologist had succeeded in demonstrating a degree of psychological reality for this aspect of our work.

Following this Guilfordian direction, there soon emerged a spate of research in what came to be called "creative thinking"—Getzels and Jackson (1962) were among the first in this, I believe, soon followed by Paul Torrance and Ram Gupta (1964), whose work became widely popular. Across this same time period one could follow the evolution of Bruner's ideas, which began with a most formal behavioral approach in the study of perception (Bruner and Postman 1947), and marched in steady step to a disciplined, but clearly cognitive assessment of concept development in his work *A Study of Thinking* (Bruner *et al.* 1956). Bruner's work prepared him to undertake a leadership role at the time of educational reform that followed Russia's successful launching of the rocket Sputnik. His *Process of Education*

(1960), a report on the Woods Hole conference, was to have wide influence. In this work one finds no support for teaching as conditioning but instead a clear demand for the exercise of creative and critical thinking in every dimension of the curriculum. The so-called "new math" and "new science" programs of the 1960s are the somewhat over-zealous outcome of this changed direction in psychological thought.

In the early Sixties, Piaget was rediscovered, and the massive work of the great Genevan began at last to be read, studied, challenged, and interpreted from an educational viewpoint (Hunt 1961; Flavell 1963; Laurendeau and Pinard 1968; Almy 1966). It may be instructive for those who did not live through this period as students to learn that Piaget was accorded but a single page in a developmental psychology text that I was assigned in 1957. (The first paragraph or two told what Piaget had found; the rest told why it was nonsense.) I find it interesting also to recall that in my first doctoral seminar, 1960, which was devoted to linguistics, the work of Noam Chomsky was not included. Roger Brown was our visiting scholar that fall and would in the next decade spearhead a major line of research in language acquisition based upon Chomsky's theory (Brown 1973), yet then I do not remember Chomsky's name being mentioned. Thus, do scientific revolutions filter but slowly to the surface of academia, and even more slowly into the classroom.

☐ Noam Chomsky and B. F. Skinner

In 1957, B. F. Skinner, distinguished professor of psychology at Harvard, published in his retirement year the now well-known work *Verbal Behavior*. In the same year, Noam Chomsky, then a young Harvard linguist, published his first book, *Syntactic Structures* (1957). They were very different works. In the former, Skinner brought the full power of behavioral theory to an explication of the acquisition and use of human language. In the latter, Chomsky applied mathematical logic to a critique of two major theories of grammar and advanced a third, his own generative transformational theory, which he considered superior to the others in simplicity and power. Lyons (1970) has observed that Chomsky's position in *Syntactic Structures* was within the bounds of Bloomfieldian linguistics; it was an abstract formulation and made no assertions about "meaning." The force of Chomsky's position became more clear, however, in his now celebrated review of Skinner's work in 1959.

Chomsky attacked Skinner's work first on psychological grounds. He did not deny the principles of operant conditioning as they had been demonstrated in animal studies and in controlled laboratory settings, nor did he question that such principles might describe some aspects of language use. He challenged absolutely, however, the possibility of applying such constructs as stimulus-response, habit strength and the like to a description of human language competence and the phenomenon of language acquisition. Chomsky argued that in order to account for language learning Skinner had extended the constructs of behavioral theory to a degree that they were neither observable nor measurable.

These depleted constructs must, Chomsky argued, be seen to stand in fundamental contradiction to the theory under which they were advanced. He adduced a very large number of examples for each component of the behavioral armory to support his case. His observation regarding reinforcement is but one illustration. "We find a heavy appeal to automatic self-reinforcement. Thus, 'a man talks to himself because of the reinforcement he receives.'" (Chomsky 1959, p. 30). Defined this way, Chomsky reasoned, the construct of reinforcement amounts to no more than the vaguely defined mentalistic language of everyday use. It is equivalent to saying that a man talks to himself because he "wishes to" or "wants to" or "likes to" and so lacks either explanatory power or scientific interest.

As an alternative, Chomsky proposed that serious questions about verbal behavior cannot be posed at the surface level of speech or in the chance aspects of language use. Instead, after Lashley (1929), he saw the reality of language as inherent in those grammatical structures and transformation rules, including phonology, that mediate between meaning and speech. He held that it was in this domain that the language user knows and is thus able to generate and comprehend an infinitely varying language surface. If I may hazard a metaphor, the surface of speech is by Chomsky's formulation a phantom like the wind, whose reality lies in those complex universal forces that generate it. A study of the wind on the basis of when and whence and how hard it blows, alone, cannot attain explanatory power and must at last diffuse into myth. In effect, Chomsky reasoned that the mentalistic decay of the Skinnerian constructs was an inevitable outcome of his focus upon the surface of language which like the wind is but an unsubstantial aspect of reality.

The finite set of rules, complex but innately knowable, was the generative transformational grammar that Chomsky advanced in *Syntactic Structures*. At this point, it is clear that he had moved altogether from the behavioristic Bloomfieldian position and was committed to a theory of language both radically new and powerfully reasoned. By the mid-1960s, his ideas would sweep the field of linguistics and integrate this discipline forcibly with the full range of human sciences and with philosophy.

☐ Transformational Generative Grammar

At the heart of the Chomskian design is the distinction made between language competence and language use, between *the language* and what at any time may be said. Also central to his model is the assertion that a reliable statement about competence can be made on the basis of what a speaker of the language can say and can interpret. It may be shown that human beings, though they vary from one to another and from culture to culture, have nonetheless a finite though mobile vocabulary or lexicon. The dictionary has a final page. But this is not true for the sentences we speak. It can be shown logically and intuitively, we know, that we are able to produce and understand an infinite number of different sentences. Thus words are limited, sentences limitless. This condition implies, of course, that an essentially creative component is a fact of language. Any model for its design must contain an access for will and option (Chomsky 1968).

Chomsky argues further that language is a species-specific phenomenon. There are no intact human beings who do not have language, nor do monkeys, bees, or jackdaws have a language in any way comparable to it. Moreover, he notes that the young of every culture acquire the mother tongue with great speed, yet without formal instruction and on the basis of obviously incomplete and imperfect data. Finally he observes that language is acquired at much the same rate and in much the same way in all language groups and cultures.

A theory of language competence must, according to Chomsky, take these facts about language into account and may not attribute to the human mind a capacity less complex than will meet these empirical conditions. Generative transformational grammar is one such statement.

What is attempted in this model is the formulation of a limited set of generative rules capable of accounting for all, and only possible, sentences in any language. The term generative, as Lyons (1970) has pointed out, is here used in the formal mathematical sense as in a formula in algebra. The expression $(2x + 3y - 6z = 6)$ will generate an infinite, but restricted set of values. In this way the conditions all and only are met. The number of possible sentences is infinite—but *only* those of the set or multiple sets are allowable for language in general and a given language in particular. It is held that all languages have certain rules in common—universal rules—and that some are specific to the individual language system. It is reasoned further that for all languages certain rules are obligatory, others are optional. Thus one may choose between *John hit the ball* and *The ball was hit by John* to convey roughly the same predication, but one does not produce or accept *John the ball was hit*. One can see that access is provided for freedom of will and choice.

In the Chomskian model the transformational rules lie between what is termed a surface structure of the language and a deep or base structure. The former expresses the order as it will later appear when spoken. The latter expresses the logical relationships necessary to the intended predication. This provision is crucial to the design, as it makes possible the differentiation between sentences whose surface forms are identical but whose meanings are different (and vice versa).

The well-known Chomskian example of this circumstance are the paired sentences *John is easy to please* versus *John is eager to please*. In this case, rules of wide generality express the shift of John as object in the former to John as subject in the latter. In similar fashion the rules may express the ambiguity of a phrase like *American history teacher*, another often-used Chomsky example. Here different relationships at the base structural level will dictate which rules for stress must subsequently be used to convey a quite unambiguous statement at the final level of speech itself—American History teacher versus American history teacher.

A schema of Chomsky's model may be described thus. What he terms categorical and lexical components are first mapped to the nodes of the base syntactic structure. This may be expressed in a tree diagram or in mathematical brackets that denote the functional relations of the predication. Lexical items are represented by elements described by phonetic entries which contain all and only those featural characteristics of the word not otherwise predictable by semantic, syntactic, and phonological rules. Next, the application of the appropriate transformations generates the surface structure which will now contain the words expressed in their phonological base form—i.e., in the order they will be spoken. Phonological rules generate the final contours of the spoken sentence.

Chomsky does not assert that his schema is the only possible one or that his set of complex transformational rules are final and complete. (I might add, however, that he is a fierce defender of his judgment in these matters, and he is well qualified to be so.) Nonetheless, he has continued to revise his formulations, particularly in the manner of treating the semantic element and in defining his position on the relationship between language and predicative thought. During the past decade a new and able group of linguists have argued that Chomsky placed too great an emphasis on syntax to the neglect of meaning. In their alternative formulations a semantic scan is seen to hold the central initiating position and from it syntactic and phonological adjustments flow, but incidentally. These too are productive models, though I think them faulty. Interesting research in language and reading comprehension deriving from these models is yielding some of the most informative findings yet achieved in this perplexing area (Frederickson 1975; Kintch 1974; Anderson 1977). I think it may fairly be said, however, that these competing models are variations on a theme which Chomsky's original work first introduced to American science.

It is important to recognize that these linguistic models are abstract. They are designs from which serious and testable questions may derive, but they do not require in and of themselves psychological reality. They are an expression meeting the conditions of language competence and are to be preferred to the degree that they do so in a manner that is economical and intuitively sound. A formulation, for example, that attributed to the "mind" the properties of a modern computer would be rejected intuitively. As one scholar put it, "The mind hasn't got that much energy," which I believe is quite literally true. On the other hand, one can see a continuing problem of parsimony in achieving the best balance between complexity and number of rules.

In Chomsky's model the rules are extremely complex, and it is for this reason in part that he argues the basis of human language must be innate. The language data available to the young child are incomplete and insufficient to support such complex learning on the basis of imitation, induction, and generalization. Instead, Chomsky would characterize the acquisition of language by a child as the realization of an innate language potential in response to the language to which he is exposed. This stand by Chomsky was shocking to many scholars who had been reared in the behaviorist tradition (Carroll 1965). Innateness is clearly a scrap-basket term that may explain everything and nothing. Yet it seems to me in this case both valid and useful. Does innateness not stand here as an abstract expression that posits a neurological design unique to human beings and fit for language?

☐ Some Effects of the Model

At all events, the Chomskian revolution has proved a revolution indeed. The serious study of language on the basis of surface events and conditioning principles has well nigh ceased. In his 1967 Berkeley lectures (Chomsky 1968; see also Chomsky 1966), Chomsky seated his model in the Cartesian tradition and related it to the linguistic writings of the philosophers of that period. Today, in fact, Neo-Platonists (Weimer 1973) speak unabashedly of soul and of free will. The triviality of the measurable and the significance of the yet unmeasured is recognized in a way that was simply unimaginable twenty years ago.

When Huey (1908) spoke of reading as advancing by a projection outward from the "mind," he did so on the basis of empirical evidence. Subjects could identify words as rapidly as letters, and phrases as rapidly as words. They could identify words at levels of illumination at which individual letters could not be discerned. Clearly this perceptual "competence" must be taken into account. (To the best of my knowledge it was not seriously investigated again until the late 1960s [Wheeler 1970]). Rather interestingly, Huey (1908) had added a footnote assuring the reader that he did not intend, by using the word "mind," to speak mentalistically. He had confidence in the radical empiricist doctrines of William James and believed that these conditions could be explained in radical empiricist terms (Huey 1908; p. 106). Nonetheless, for clarity he felt he must adopt a position of dualism, and he argued that this whole area of word perception would have to be thought through anew. Huey argued, in short, that it was absolutely necessary to take into account what the mind did, whether or not one could at present measure it. As we have seen, the advances of reading research and methodological reform for the next seventy-five years were largely limited to the measurables, and the "hard" facts about the mind were neglected. A major effect of the Chomskian revolution has been to renew the focus of science upon mind and to shift from a preoccupation with surface measures to a curiosity about "the contribution of the child to language learning" (DeCecco 1967, p. 339).

One important line of research that stemmed directly and quite naturally from Chomsky's theory was the study of language development. Heretofore, much careful work had been done in this area that resulted largely in typologies (Gesell 1940, for example), norms, frequency counts, and the like. Now, guided by a theory that postulated the acquisition not simply of words but of a grammar, researchers sought to make sense of early language behavior in terms of such an underlying syntax (Bellugi and Brown 1964; Berko 1958; Menyuk 1968). From this work it has been shown that children at the babbling stage articulate all possible speech sounds and, long before beginning to talk, gradually drop away those phonations not used in the mother tongue. The first single-word utterances are interpreted, in the context of the child's behavior, not as words simply, but as sentences. Thus my son's first word, "chicken," was produced in purposeful tones as he trotted across the lawn to the henyard and could not be judged simply imitation, echo, or parroting but a predication of intent—"I will go and look at the chickens"—which he did in fact do, clinging to the wire and gazing with obvious satisfaction. (He is presently, I might add, a reasonably competent amateur ornithologist.)

In the two-word constructions of early language—"milk allgone," "Daddy allgone," "Granny allgone"—a simple grammar of open and pivot class was reasoned. Recently, some questions about the adequacy of this formulation have been raised. Nonetheless, it still holds, I believe, that this general pattern is common across widely differing language groups, and this manner of speaking is clearly different from that which the child hears. Adults use "baby talk" now and then, but seldom to each other. Moreover, they learn it from their children, not the other way around. These observations tend to support a belief in cognitive and linguistic universals and in the idea that the child's grammar is constructed progressively rather than achieved simply through imitation, association, and generalization (C. Chomsky 1970, 1972; Templeton 1976).

One interesting finding in this body of research relates to children's use of strong English verbs and the weak or inflected forms (Berko 1958). Initially, children are found to acquire the higher frequency strong verbs and to use them correctly—for example, go, went, gone. At a later date, inflections begin to be used—as in walk and walked. Then a remarkable thing happens. The previously correctly used strong verb now occurs in the familiar incorrect form of childhood as Daddy goed to the store. Here is striking evidence that it is the rules, not the words, that are learned and that these are forged from the child out and not from the language in. One may infer from the example given here that an overgeneralization of rule has occurred from weak verb to strong verb. Eventually this well-reasoned error will resolve itself; yet while it endures, we have the phenomenon of a child using a language form that simply does not exist in his natural language environment. Further, one may see in this design a circumstance in which the child's error provides evidence of a positive cognitive grasp of language. It was this kind of observation that first led me to believe that a study of children's spelling *errors* might eventually lead to some understanding about a progressive conceptual knowledge of English orthography.

Is English Spelling Regular?

☐ Autonomous Phonemics

Before turning to studies of children's word knowledge it is necessary to trace briefly the ways in which the question of orthographic regularity has been studied by psycholinguists and to show in what sense the revised opinion of a relatively high degree of regularity has been reached. Bloomfield's influence led to a revived appreciation of the alphabetic character of English spelling. Through the use of his more refined linguistic terminology, a far more adequate statement was achieved of what was regular on the basis of surface phoneme-grapheme correspondence. An extension of Bloomfield's position, which has been termed Autonomous Phonemics, was intentionally behavioral—concerned with the association of classifiable sound groups (phonemes) with letter and letter groups (graphemes). Phonemes in spoken English were deemed to be established by the frequency of their occurrence quite independently of meaning. Though I think many do not realize it, this is the theory asserted when it is claimed that reading is decoding.

Working under the framework of the Bloomfieldian theory, Hanna and Moore (1953) made a close analysis of 3,000 words from a spelling list. They concluded that eighty percent of the phonemes were represented consistently by the same letter or letters in more than half of the occurrences of these phonemes in words.

Thomas Horn (1957) disagreed sharply, pointing out that in a list of 10,000 words, one third of them had more than one allowable pronunciation. Thus, regular correspondence for one speaker would be irregular for another. In addition he noted that in the average American dictionary, fifty percent of the words contain silent letters, a condition that the Hanna and Moore study did not take into account. Horn concluded that English spelling was far less regular than linguistic investigators tended to claim.

Somewhat later, Hanna *et al.* (1966) conducted a more sophisticated analysis making use of a computer analog. Instead of treating phoneme-grapheme correspondence in isolation, they took into account both the position of the element in the syllable and whether or not the syllable was stressed. They used as a base the standard pronunciation given in the *Webster's New Collegiate Dictionary* (1961).

With the application of these additional criteria, Hanna *et al.* were able to demonstrate a sustantially higher level of orthographic regularity. They concluded that almost all consonant sounds, and some vowel sounds, were represented by one grapheme over eighty percent of the time. When the computer analog was directed to spell the 17,000 words of the Thorndike and Lorge List (1944), it attained a score of about forty-nine percent representation.

This work was to meet with heavy criticism. Limitations were found in the word lists employed, particularly by the absence of derived and inflected forms in the Thorndike and Lorge List (Roberts 1967). Also, reminiscent of Horn's earlier argument, Roberts held that a single standard failed to account for common dialectic variation. Reed (1976) insisted that this work was flawed by its "failure to view English phonology consistently as part of the total structure of English grammar" (Reed 1976, p. 208). In this contention one sees the influence of Chomsky and Halle's (1968) very different theoretical position, one that denies the possibility of reaching meaningful descriptions of orthography under the limitation of an autonomous phonemic model.

□ Morphophonemic Theory

The work of Venezky (1967) stands, as it were, midway on the continuum between the behaviorist and the cognitive or psycholinguistic theory of phonology. It stems from the traditional morphophonemic theory (Swadesh and Voegelin 1939) which treated the meaning units of language, the morphemes, as the base from which the phonetic surface might be reached indirectly through the application of a series of rules.

Venezky applied morphophonemic theory to a study of a body of 20,000 English words in an attempt to determine the nature of those rules which might generate spelling to sound correspondence. In his analysis of the surface patterns of orthography Venezky proposed a set of functional units that predict sound. These he then divided into the subcategories of relational units and markers. Since in English, *rs* never occurs at the beginning of a syllable, it would not qualify as a functional unit in that position. Similarly, *v* alone does not end a word, e.g., *have*, not *hav*, is here the functional unit. A relational unit is exemplified by the *th* in *this*, *thing*, or *that*. Here the phonemes /ð/ and /θ/ are not predictable from the *t* and *h* separately. By markers are meant those letters, often, but not always unpronounced, which serve to indicate how other letters or letter clusters are pronounced. Examples of this might be the silent *e* in *bone*, "governing" the long sound of *o*, or the pronounced *i* in *city* "controlling" the /s/ sound for *c*.

To this much more powerful surface analysis, Venezky proposed a four-stage process leading to a predictable pronunciation of the functioning units. First, a morphemic scan divided the word into its meaning units. By this means, the *ph* in *shepherd* would be divided between the *p* and *h*, thus ruling out the appropriate choice of *ph* /f/ in *Phillip*. At the second stage, the relational units were mapped into their phonemic representation on a one-to-one basis. Next, at a morphemic level were applied syntactic, semantic, and phonological rules that might modify the previous mapping in various ways. For example, the form class "verb" versus "noun" would generate *record'* instead of *re'cord*. Similarly, phonological rules might serve and govern the silent *g* in *signing* in contrast to its sounded form in *signal*. Finally the phonetic naturally spoken form of the word was realized.

By applying such intermediate rules between the morphological base and the phonetic surface, a far more orderly picture of English orthography emerged, and many of the limitations plaguing the direct phoneme-grapheme correspondence analyses were overcome. In the sense that rules are involved, Venezky's model is cognitive in design. On the other hand, the fact that *e* serves as a marker or that *rs* does not begin a syllable must be taken as quite arbitrary. In this latter sense, the Venezky design is more behaviorally oriented, less a treatise on competence than an analysis of abstract order on the basis of the facts of performance.

☐ Phonological Theory

Phonological theory, as developed by Chomsky and Halle (1968), is quite different from the morphophonemic model advanced by Venezky. There is a fundamental disagreement between the two positions, and in each the assertion made for regularity or optimality of English spelling rests on a substantially different base. For Venezky, underlying rules were found to generate a correspondence between functional letter units and sound. Generative phonological theory denies the reality of any such correspondence (except as an artifact of linguistic analysis) and reasons instead that the correspondence holds between the orthographic surface and the base lexical form of the word.

It is important to recognize that the theoretical and procedural gulf that separates the work of Chomsky and Venezky does not invalidate the commonality of their findings—that English spelling is more optimal and orderly than it seems. Note too that this very same conclusion has been reached from yet a third position, that of the historical linguist Bradley (1918). It is the confluence of these findings that has required and indeed made possible a reassessment of childrens' knowledge of English words.

In Chomsky's model, lexical elements are mapped initially to the base-phrase structure. These elements are represented by phonetic notations but *are not at this stage sounds*. Instead, they are abstract codings denoting the minimal number of featural elements of the word not otherwise predictable by the application of those transformations and adjustment rules required in any particular sentence in which that word may be used. In the sentence *John performed a courageous act*, the word *courageous* is reasoned to require the following lexical elements at the base level: /korɘge/ + the formant ADJ (adjective). Transformation and the adjustment rules then realize the phonological representation: /korɘge s/, at the level of surface structure. In addition, it is held that such entries are tagged or marked by their derivational class (such as the word *romance*) and that such knowledge is part of the ideal speaker/listener, reader/writer's knowledge of his language.

This assertion is crucial for the distinction made between Venezky's model and that of Chomsky and Halle. For the latter, markers like the silent *e* in *courageous*, for example, have meaning not at the surface but at the base, where that element is or is not required by a set of phonological readjustment rules appertaining to that word as a function of its particular derivational class. Thus, in phonological theory, the *e* is not a surface requirement but a base requirement (courage), if a finite set of phonological rules is to generate the appropriate spoken form. In this model one sees a set of phonological rules of wide generality mediating between sound and lexical base, a notation that contains all and only those features that are required. What is remarkable from the point of view of orthography is the fact that the derived base form matches "optimally," in a remarkably consistent manner, the standard English spelling.

Clearly, Chomsky's and Halle's model is a powerful one. Their design accounts for the production and apprehension of meaning across widely varying dialectic groups. It also expresses the means by which written language has the capacity to endure over time. We may read Shakespeare today and understand him, though doubtless the speech, i.e., the dialect and inflection, of that period would be most difficult for us to follow. Even further, it may be shown that phonological rules encompass the Great Vowel Shift in English as expressed in the stable relationships for words like *divine-divinity, serene-serenity*. Here the root is retained visually, constant across the tense/lax vowel pairings of modern English, which Moore (1951) has pointed out were paired in speech quite differently in middle English.

In the light of generative-phonological theory, written English may be seen to be abstract but not chaotic. Its regularity lies at this lexical base which is linked to a necessarily fluid surface by a finite though mobile rule system. It may be reasoned, moreover, that all written languages must in some measure be abstract. It is also probable, I think, that the evolution of different writing systems may express the characteristics of their particular grammar by the position at which they lie on this concrete-abstract continuum. I find it difficult to accept the notion, for example, that Chinese orthography is bad, English better, and perhaps reformed Spanish orthography best. Indeed, one outcome of phonological theory must be to achieve a far more sensitive grasp of the issues of language reform and its implications for world literacy.

As Charles Read (1976) has pointed out, speech, as recorded on a spectograph, where every tonal nuance is recorded, is altogether unreadable. A phonetic alphabet, of course, is an abstraction of the elements of speech and, in the hands of skilled linguists, may record speech quite narrowly. Such a device, however, would be most unwieldy as a writing system. Once again there is more information given than is needed; it simply gets in the way of a swift prediction of meaning. The initial teaching alphabet (*i t a*) of Sir James Pitman (1969) is a further abstraction, less concrete than the International Phonetic Alphabet, less abstract than English. Finally, we may follow the continuum downward to include reformed Spanish, perhaps English, the ideograph of Eastern languages, the pictograph, and finally probably pictures.

One can see quite easily in this array, I think, the series of trade-offs as they may affect efficiency in the production and apprehension of meaning by graphic means. Nor does a written language hold constantly to its own fixed position but may move upward toward speech, as was contrived for Spanish, or downward as occurred for English when the tense vowel forms shifted in the spoken language. Moreover, in all languages, different kinds of graphic abstractions are found useful and are employed for suitable purposes. The international sign system reaches the widest audience and stamps its message home most conveniently. We find "$" a handy logograph at times and usually resort to some form of phonetics to convey a dialect if we choose to do so. For the mass of written communication, however, there is some general area near the mean where maximum efficiency lies. Phonological theory defines written English in such terms and reveals in the spelling system a propriety and power wholly obscured from a surface view.

□ Limitations of a Competence Model

It is important at this juncture to emphasize that phonological theory, as I have treated it up to this point, is focused upon competence, upon the abstract knowledge of an idealized mature language user. This model does not in itself predict what the child might know about his language at any particular time, nor by what stages he might come to acquire such knowledge. Least of all does this theory provide ready inferences about how reading and spelling should be taught. Chomsky (1970) gives clear warning on this point.

. . .the study of sound structure is in a state of intensive development; no one can say with any security what will be the fate of the conventional wisdom of today. The subject is alive, exciting, and changing. The second point is that, even if we had achieved near certainty on some basic issues of phonology, it is by no means obvious that conclusions of any importance would follow for the study of reading and teaching of reading (p. 3).

In this same article, Chomsky permits himself one cautious speculation about phonological development and its possible psychological realization.

It is by no means obvious that a child of six has mastered this phonological system in full. He may not yet have been presented with the evidence that determines the general structure of this system. A similar question arises in the case of an adult who is not immersed in the literary culture. It would not be surprising to discover that the child's intuitive organization of the sound system continues to develop and deepen as his vocabulary is enriched and as his use of language extends to wider intellectual domains and more complex functions. Hence, the sound system that corresponds to the orthography may itself be a late intellectual product. Furthermore, we have no understanding of how tentative conclusions about the sound system, constructed by the child at one stage of his development, may affect the interpretation he gives to data and his effort to deepen this analysis as his knowledge of language grows.

For various reasons, then, it may turn out that the psychologically real representation for the child changes and deepens with age, approaching the adult phonology with increasing maturity and experience with language. Serious investigation of these questions is far from easy, but it should shed much light on problems of speech perception and production and general problems of how language is used, and perhaps, indirectly on the problems of literacy as well (pp. 17–18).

Charles Read's work, to be discussed later, focused on just such a psychological reality of phonology among young children. And following him, our own studies would approach these matters in the more applied setting of the classroom.

An Early Study of Word Knowledge

Our initial work in the study of children's spelling began in 1970, but it should be understood that at that time my grasp of psycholinguistics was most fragile and paltry. It would be some years before my students and I could, from our layman position as educators, begin to comprehend the sweep of these theories and their possible implications for educational research. I had read the year before Chomsky's *Language and Mind* (1968) and understood parts of it; also James Deese's *Psycholinguistics* (1970). I had read some of Venezky's work as well but was unable to see then the distinction between his approach and that of Chomsky's. Nonetheless, it seemed clear to me that the proposition that English spelling was arbitrary could no longer be held. Instead, I felt that a major aspect of this facility must be covert and cognitive, and had probably been much neglected in our pedagogical efforts. It was my hunch that an examination of children's spelling errors in a creative writing setting might, like the errors in language acquisition, provide evidence from which some dimensions of this progressive conceptualization of word might be inferred.

As described earlier, I had had extended experience working with children, following a language experience approach, one in which they were encouraged to write just as soon as they had a modest sight vocabulary and could form the letters of the alphabet. When they did not know how to spell a word and could not conveniently find it, they were directed to make their best guess and proceed with their essay. I felt that this setting provided an unusual opportunity to study invented spellings in order to see if we could make any sense of what the children were doing. Accordingly, I arranged to draw a sample of one week's production from all the children in twenty-two first grade classrooms in Prince George County, Maryland, with whose teachers I had been working as a consultant for several years.

I was curious, in addition to studying spelling, to examine the characteristics of the children's sight vocabularies and to gain some index of their productivity as storytellers and writers. I felt our findings might be of interest in these latter areas because it is often assumed that first graders cannot write at all and because their sight word holdings were likely to be quite different from the controlled lists typically built into standard basal reader series.

We found (Henderson *et al.* 1972) that the mean number of stories produced that week for all classrooms was 2.3, with a range of 0 to 4.4. The mean number of running words was 75.9, with a range of 0 to 176.0. This seems to us to provide fairly convincing evidence that indeed first graders can be productive if given the chance to do so. With regard to word bank holdings, the classroom means were found comparable to the typical number planned for inclusion in basal readers by mid-year. The mean holding was 91.4, with a range of 32.6 to 192.6. As may be inferred, the range for individual children was from one or two words up to well over 400. With these data, one gets a good sense of the individualization of instruction possible with this kind of approach. Children were not all "doing the same thing at their own rate." They were doing the best they could and advancing as they could. Some were dictating brief phrases and sentences and as yet recalling few words on a reliable basis. Others were writing well-constructed accounts and remembering nearly every new word that they met. This, it seems to me, was as it should be.

To study the characteristics of the words in the word banks we took a random sample of twenty-five children from the 594, pooled their word bank holdings, and tallied these against a one to six scale derived from the Thorndike and Lorge "general" list of word frequency per written words. About fifty-six percent of the words fell roughly into the set of the most frequently occurring words in the language, level 1. The remaining words were about evenly distributed across the scale, with two percent falling outside the list altogether.

The fear some teachers have that children must be drilled to learn high frequency "function words" appears from these findings to be unfounded. Occurrence of these words in natural language is clearly sufficient to insure their early mastery on a recognition basis. Moreover, if a rich experience with words is a necessary condition for advancing phonological knowledge (Chomsky 1970; C. Chomsky 1970), then one must consider the distribution of known words across the lower frequency strata a particularly felicitous circumstance for these children. Their experience was not limited to high frequency words alone.

In order to examine the errors in creative writing, we subdivided the children in the random sample according to a rating of their word bank holdings (high, middle, and low), then pooled and recorded all errors next to the correct form for each group. This was a crude way indeed to begin, but it was the best we could think then to do. Simply by inspection, the three groups spelled largely by consonant fragments, but these fragments were almost invariably correct. In the middle group, vowels were almost always included, and it was among vowels and certain consonants that most errors occurred. Finally, in the top groups, errors occurred quite often in the misuse of a vowel marker—SOPE for *soap*, for example. On the face of it, these children's errors were not random and mindless—something was going on in their heads.

Invented Spellings and Phonological Theory

It was at this point that I came upon an article by Charles Read in the *Harvard Educational Review* titled "Pre-school Children's Knowledge of English Phonology" (1971). It was an exciting moment for me, for suddenly I realized that a door had opened to a systematic study of children's concepts of speech sounds and written words. A linguist, steeped in the phonological theories of Chomsky and Halle, Read had the genius to see that a study of children's invented spellings might make possible certain inferences about their phonological systems in contrast to that predicted for the mature literate adult. He was to test in fact the hypothesis to this effect by Edward Sapir (1925) which had hitherto been deemed mentalistic and quite untestable.

Read's pre-school subjects were twenty children from ages three and a half to six, some from a Montessori school, some simply at home, where they were allowed to experiment with writing and encouraged to do s early. For the most part they were told correct spellings only when they asked. As Read examined their productions, he was able to discern a good number of errors which occurred consistently among the children and which changed progressively and consistently across age. Far more important, he was able to interpret and make sense of these consistencies in the light of phonological theory.

☐ Vowel Spellings

Regarding vowels, Read was able to show that when the long form was called for, children spelled it by its letter name, but without those markers which commonly accompany it in standard spelling. Thus *came* was spelled KAM; *table*, TABL; *rose*, ROS; and so on. The short vowels, however, posed a far more complex problem. Since there is no letter name to match these sounds, the children could have omitted them altogether or invented a new letter for them or substituted a convenient consonant like *f* /ef/ for the sound /e / in *net*. But they did not do so. Instead, they substituted for the missing element the long vowel that was closest to that short sound both acoustically and by point of articulation. Thus, *fish* was spelled FES; *pen*, PAN; *got*, GIT. One sees in this finding clear evidence that children accept the abstract nature of alphabetic writing, i.e., that it is not a simple one-symbol/one-sound system but that phonemes may be expected to be grouped and substituted one for another on the basis of common properties or perceived similarities. The particular strategy applied by these children to the short vowel is incredibly interesting and appears to plumb deep into the history of language. To see how wonderful it really is we may examine the sounds represented by the letters *e* and *i* in greater detail.

By place of articulation these are represented thus:

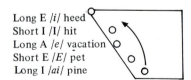

Long E /i/ heed
Short I /I/ hit
Long A /e/ vacation
Short E /E/ pet
Long I /ai/ pine

In standard English we pair (use the same letter) long *i* /ai/ with short *i* /I/ as in p*i*ne and p*i*n. This relationship is governed by a sequence of phonological rules which hold constant the lexical (and spelled) form in such terms as div*i*ne and div*i*nity, comb*i*ne-comb*i*nation, mal*i*gn-mal*i*gnity, and so on. Historically, however, these words were not pronounced as they are today. Long *i* was pronounced /i/ (as in team) as it is still in French and German. In the Great Vowel Shift of the 14th century two things happened to the pronunciation of English tense vowels. First, these vowels added a y or w glide and became diphthongs. Second, they lifted upward from their companion short vowel to the next higher position, with the effect that the highest vowel i (then pronounced like our present long e) swung around to the lowest position, /ə/ + glide y or long i, as it is spoken today.

Now look again at what Read's children did in selecting an appropriate vowel letter for the sound of short i /l/ as in *fish*. They chose e, FES. They formed a substitution category on the basis of a phonetic relationship which, after a change in the pronunciation of long vowels, is no longer honored orthographically. In an amazingly consistent manner, Read's children selected a for short e, e for short i, i for short o, and o for short u. Truly such a finding is uncanny. And it would have been impossible to discern, I think, in the absence of phonetic theory. Clearly, these children brought to the task of beginning writing a remarkable phonological knowledge. Equally clearly, that knowledge was incomplete, for it did not include vowel shift.

☐ Affricates

Read succeeded in supporting this conviction in a parade of further findings each reflecting tacit strategies and conceptual groupings of the phonemic sequences of words as represented by letters. For the condition when d and t precede r (in everyday classroom language, the tr and dr blends), children frequently elected to disregard the d and t and to represent the affriction instead. Thus *train* was spelled CHRAN and *drive*, JRIV.

Of this circumstance Read (1971) observes:

> Because the affrication before /r/ is predictable, standard spelling ignores it, using the lexical representatives tr and dr. Evidently, the children perceive the affrication. Not knowing the lexical representations, they must choose between the known spellings T/D or CH/J for these intermediate cases. They consistently choose on the basis of affrication, abstracting from the difference in place-of-articulation. They always match affricate /t/ and /d/ with the affricates that correspond in voicing—/c/ and /j/, respectively (p. 94).

☐ Flaps

In words where the letter t was bounded by vowels as in *water*, Read found that children initially would render t as a d, WOODR. Phonetically the choice is a sound one, for in this condition, called a flap, the tongue taps the alveolar ridge, and the sound is voiced, making it in fact closer to d than t. Curiously, this decision is soon abandoned by children, and d is replaced by the standard form t. "The child who wrote LADR and PRETE at age three and a half or four wrote LATR, SESTR, and PREDE at age five" (p. 97). That children do this consistently, i.e., replace the voiced flap which "should be" *t* with *d* is evidence, Read argues, that "spelling is 'rule-governed' behavior" (p. 97).

Regarding the nasals, /m/ /n/, Read found that while these were commonly represented correctly in their initial and final position, NIT (*night*), WAN (*when*) for example, they were typically omitted when they occurred before a consonant. BOPY for *bumpy*, ED for *end*, SIC for *sink*. And here again he was able to provide a rationale for why this should be so. It was not that children could not distinguish between *wet* and *went* but rather that the preconsonantal nasal in this position is different from initial or final nasals—"bunp" must be pronounced *bump* any way you try it.

☐ Vocalic Consonants

A remarkably persistent strategy in children's invented spellings was shown by Read to occur in words like *tiger, little,* and *wagon,* which they rendered TIGR, LITL, WAGN. Here the vowel is omitted in these second syllables, though the same is not done for the reduced vowel followed by a true consonant, or obstruent, as in the second syllable of *circus*, SRKIS. Read concludes that children must tacitly classify these syllabic consonants differently from the others for which distinction in fact there is sound phonetic reason. In this case, i.e., LITL, as with the preconsonantal nasals, the vowel is redundant. Since the trend in learning conventional spelling is precisely toward the economic reduction of the mass of phonetic detail at the surface, one would expect this overgeneralization to persist, and it did in Read's data.

☐ Inflections

By following the children's progressive spelling of past tense forms, Read was able to trace the evolution of a morphological strategy in a most interesting way. Initially, children spelled the past tense with a straightforward phonetic rendering—MARED for *married*, LAFFT for *laughed*, HALPT for *helped*. Next came a change to rendering the regularly inflected forms with a constant *d* while treating the non-regular forms differently. Thus they wrote WALKD for *walked*, but KUT for *caught*. Of this circumstance Read makes the following point:

> A uniform-D may appear for both /d/ and /t/ in regular past forms long before the standard -ed. These spellings are certainly not copied from adults in any simple sense. The development from phonetic to morphophonemic is not a direct move from phonetic to adult spelling;

rather, there is a dramatic change in the type of (non-adult) spelling the child creates (p. 107).

Finally, in the spellings of plurals, Read notes what he terms a special case. Here, from the beginning, children rendered the varying /s/ /z/ /iz/ with s alone, for example, SOKS (socks), LADYS (ladies), RASIS (races). Rejecting the idea that children cannot distinguish between these sounds, for the evidence of their perceptivity is abundant throughout, he concludes that they have early on abstracted away this noninformation-bearing phonetic difference and elected the single rendering s. "This conclusion (on the children's part)," Read notes, "would be another over-generalization but not for plurals, the most common examples" (p. 109).

☐ Conclusions

Taken together, Read's work at this point strongly supported Chomsky's intuition that the phonological knowledge of the literate adult advanced as a function of experiences with written language. The complex rules mediating between speech and some phonological base appeared indeed to be incomplete in young children. They did not treat vowels in accordance with the fact that our long vowel has undergone a shift. On the other hand, these children demonstrated an incredible sense of how written language must work—that it is not simply a surface code of serial phoneme-grapheme matches. Instead, they acted upon it generating rules to economize and reach inward toward an increasingly abstract form. With incredible sensitivity to the nuances of the phonetic surface (their minds were not yet hardened by the categorical certainties of adulthood), they tried likely avenues for the creation of a workable written form, one which uses a single symbol for more than one sound, as most alphabetical orthographies do. Just as in their earlier acquisition of spoken language, when principles were newly and only partly grasped, they were often over-generalized. Thus, they spelled fuzzy, FASE, for a while, until a fuller conceptualization was realized. So too was tiger spelled TIGR and bumpy, BOPE, for the system under which they functioned (i.e., their present state of phonological knowledge) required that and nothing else.

So here in my story of spelling it may appear that the end has been reached in the middle. But that was not really so. I have written with great certainty about what Read's children did with their invented spellings, and so indeed did he, but he was and is far too good a scholar to have urged more from his data than it would endure. In the following years he was to fill out, tabulate, and test the probable truth of these complex choices that young writers make. In addition he would design and carry through a series of formal experiments pinpointing the categorical preferences of children for related phoneme units and show what changes occurred as they advanced toward literacy. This work is beautifully presented in Read's 1975 monograph, *Children's Categorization of Speech Sounds*. In 1970 Read discovered the way. Much work remained to be done.

The Virginia Studies of Word Knowledge

4

An Exploratory Study

Our work began by going back to school. It was necessary that we learn phonetics and at least the principles of phonological theory. In addition we needed to think carefully about our responsibility and the limitations of such an enterprise. I had no wish to do poorly what a linguist could do well, though I am not adverse to dabbling and being the fool if there may be some possible value in it.

Our first step was to look again at the data that we had from the January 1971 sample. There we found a large number of errors of the kind that Read had described. These occurred particularly in the middle group of children who, though older, were presumably more similar in development to those in Read's sample. Much the same thing was found again in a second sample of seventy-five children drawn from the same data pool (Fisher 1973). Thus it began to seem very likely that the spelling decisions that Read reported for his somewhat "exceptional" (Read 1971, p. 111) preschoolers would hold true for first graders following a language experience approach in a setting where formal word study activities were being carried on.

For the following year, we (Beers and Henderson 1977) had arranged to draw samples of one week's writing from a single first-grade classroom once each month from September to May. It was our intention to follow the children's error patterns longitudinally and to test for systematic changes in these. To this end we had developed a rather large grid on which error, omission, or substitution of character by position in the word could be tallied. Happily, no such unwieldy device was needed, for it soon became clear that beginning writers made errors, except by chance, in a narrow range that could be coded on a simple record sheet. Further, it soon became evident that "eyeball" techniques would be needed before any statistical or computer-assisted effort could sensibly be made. In effect, then, we followed the advice of Kenneth Goodman who sagely had recommended such a procedure the spring before.

At this point, we selected a variety of spelling-error categories, essentially those described by Read, to be examined among the children. These included long and short vowels; syllabic *r*; inflectional endings, *ed* and *ing*; and the flap and nasals, *m* and *n*. A new tally was then composed for each category containing the most common substitutions for each child for each monthly writing sample. By "most common" was meant those substitutions occurring in more than fifty percent of the misspellings in each category each month for each child. By observing this grid we could then identify common sequences across time and among children for each error category based on the most common substitution in that category. This kind of analysis made it possible to observe certain basic spelling strategies and to trace them sequentially.

Not surprisingly, some children moved through these sequences more rapidly than others. We decided that in order not to have to deal with sequences of various time lengths, we would hold these steps constant. For example, the child who made the same initial mistake for the first three months would be lumped with children who made the same initial mistake for only two months. This allowed for a more general statement about sequential steps and inclusion of the majority of children whose writing was examined.

While somewhat better than kicking up leaves and watching them fall, our way of looking at these data most certainly did lack the precision and strict control that formal research requires. Our effort was grossly exploratory. Nonetheless, our findings did march in a most remarkable manner with those of Read, which, as noted earlier, would later be confirmed by him statistically.

It seemed to us altogether clear that children's initial errors with vowels followed a pattern of letter-name inclusion and when this was wanting, as for the short vowels, substitutions did seem to be based largely on nearness in place of articulation, *e* for short *i* and so on. The omission of preconsonantal nasals, STAP for *stamp* and the phonetic choice of *d* for *t* in the flap condition, SWEDER for *sweater*, regularly occurred in children's early spellings, as did vowel omission with syllabic consonants *l* and *r* and the use of *g* for /ŋ/ as in BRIGIG for *bringing*.

We felt convinced that Read's findings and his interpretation of them must be recognized as a very general condition influencing the progress of children as they learned about English words. Our sample was not a "rare" group of precocious preschoolers, but a relatively ordinary assemblage of first graders who were receiving direct instruction in reading and word analysis. Moreover, we began to wonder what influence this instruction, as well as other developmental factors, might have upon this perhaps deeper and more natural acquisition of word knowledge.

The issue here is complex, not simple. Let us suppose that children come to the task of learning to read and write with a readiness to relate alphabet letters to the phonemic patterns of spoken words in a progressively abstract manner. On the other hand, man is a rule-making animal. He will act on the surface of things whether we would have him do so or not. To say that the silent *e* makes the vowel long is as inevitable as to note that the sun rises in the east, however false both statements may be in a larger sense. Moreover, the data upon which vowel shift most probably depends must lie well beyond the primary years. Pedagogically it would seem that a danger could lie in allowing or encouraging too quick a closure upon surface events, the assertion of rules and the requirement of correctness, at the expense of continued exploration, error, and inner readjustment.

The Vowels A, E, and I

Our chief concern at this time was to see if we might devise a way to test for some of these sequences in a more orderly and convincing fashion and with a sample of children who were following a more typical program of reading instruction. To this end, J. Beers (1974) limited his study to the long and short vowels, *a*, *e*, and *i*, as exemplified in a twenty-four word list of high and moderate frequency single-syllable words. These he administered as a spelling test to a sample of eighty-one first graders and seventy-five second graders five times at one month intervals from December to April. The children were largely middle class, and all attended a single Charlottesville, Virginia, elementary school in which the *Ginn 360* reading series was used for instruction.

Spelling responses were scored each month on the basis of a four-point rating scale designed to reflect the progression we had found in our previous study. For short *i*, for example, no attempt = 0, letter-name strategy (substitution *i* for *e*) = 1, transition (inclusion of a marker vowel, e.g., LIAP for *lip*) = 3, and correct form = 4. For long *e* the rating used was no attempt = O, letter-name strategy (inclusion of vowel without marker) = 1, transition (inclusion of vowel plus incorrect marker) = 3, and finally correct form = 4.

The no-attempt category was important, as Read (1975) has pointed out, in order to separate, as it were, nonbehavior from an actual decision about how a vowel should be represented. Before a child knows in some manner what a word is and the letters that compose it, he is unlikely to be able to focus what phonological knowledge he may have upon a task requiring discrimination or production. I have long believed that a circumstance of this kind must underlie the poorer showing many beginning first graders make on discrimination tasks (Gibson and Levin 1975, p. 229).

The "term letter-name strategy" denotes that decision period when the invented spelling reflects the choice of a letter on the basis of its alphabet name as discerned in the word, or the substitution of an alphabet name for the nearest short vowel for which no named letter is available. Transition errors are characterized by correct vowel inclusion, but reflect a growing sensitivity to vowel markers through their incorrect selection, placement, or inclusions. For this category, of course, it is not possible really to know what underlies these choices.

One may guess that the new pairing of short and long vowels (*pit* and *pine* and *pet* and *peat*) has begun to be internalized, but one must suppose that the more complex relationships, denoted by pairs of terms like *divine-divinity* are still well beyond these primary years. Experimentation with vowel markers may reflect tacit surface analysis on the part of the child or something he was taught and misremembered or had memorized serially and forgotten. Doubtless all and more are involved, including gross frequency of occurrence, motor learning, and the like.

In Beers's study, the raters were able to categorize responses reliably. By applying Hay's sign test (1965) to the twenty-four exemplars, he also found significantly more children changing on four out of five trials in the predicted progression than not. These effects could be seen to be strongest among first graders and for lower rather than higher frequency examplars. For second graders and for high frequency words there was, not surprisingly, a high evidence of correct responses across many trials.

An analysis of variance showed significant effects for grade for all categories, while effects for time were largely centered in grade one. Effects for frequency were also largely significant, though particular exemplars often proved confounding. The word *lip*, for example, while technically a high frequency word, nonetheless seldom occurs in primary reading materials. It appeared to have been treated by children like a low rather than a high frequency exemplar. Similarly, the exemplar *week*, which appears on nearly every classroom bulletin board, was most often spelled correctly. Invented spellings, of course, can never be a "clean" variable, as is true of so much that is of great interest in education. Beers's painstaking work-up of each element of the analysis did much to clarify the major trends as reported above.

Altogether, it is my feeling that Beers succeeded quite well in demonstrating that beginning readers, regardless of method, do apply some relatively deep underlying strategies to word construction of the kind that Read had found among precocious preschoolers. Because the emergence of the letter-name strategy and change to transitional and correct form appeared to be largely accomplished in grade one, we were interested next to see if we might not find other error types that would expose similar transitions upward through the grades. In our earlier data the tense marker *ed* had not fully established itself as a morphographemic constant; thus, it seemed a likely candidate. Also, it seemed logical that the manner of handling such inflectional endings as they are added to a root word (*bat, batted, bone, boned*) would develop only gradually and come after long and short vowel patterns were reasonably stabilized.

In his conclusions Beers suggested that an analogy might lie between the use of a letter-name strategy and Piaget's concept of centration. Thus, children might be thought of at this period as fixing on the salient feature of letter and proceeding with it unidimensionally in the construction of a word. Transitional strategies, in contrast, might be conceived as two-dimensional, feature plus pattern. It was Beers's hunch that an ability to decenter, to handle more than one aspect of a task simultaneously, might be necessary to advancing word knowledge. These issues were tackled by Zutell the following year.

Decentration and Word Knowledge

Among academics today I note an increasing caution with regard to Piagetian tasks and theory, particularly when these are applied uncautiously as research variables or directed broadly to educational procedures. It is good that this is so. Piaget's clinical method does not lend itself readily to empirical research designs; moreover, his ideas have always focused on epistemology—toward a theory of knowing not a theory of learning. In some cases, his notion of stages of intellectual development has been misconstrued as normative, that is, a statement about what one ought to do at a particular time. Further, and I think more damaging, there has been a tendency to confuse the tasks with the abstract cognitive function that underlies the performance they may elicit. After prolonged and unconscionable neglect of Piaget's work, there has now been, in some cases perhaps, a too sudden and too uncritical acceptance.

Zutell (1975) focused on the developmental period which Piaget describes as marking the transition from preoperational to concrete operational thought which tends to occur roughly between the ages of five to seven years. The characteristics of this period are summarized by Zutell as follows:

> In general, Piaget's model is based on the interaction between organism and environment. In such a model it is essential that the organism actively invent structures and apply them to experience in order to comprehend it. The types of structures available mark the difference between developmental stages.
>
> In particular, in the preoperational stage the child's structures are limited to the static condition of objects so that he "centers" on a particular immediately available perceptual cue. In the operational stage, on the other hand, the child develops more general, coordinated structures permitting him to consider transformations of objects as operations which relate previous states to present ones. He is thus able to move away from isolated consideration of static perceptual information.
>
> More specifically, the difference between these two stages can be observed in the child's attempts to deal with problems of perceptual and logical part-whole relationships and with the several levels of the problem of conservation of number and quantity. In these examples the preoperational child fails to consider transforma-

tional relationships which the operational child views as essential to the proper solution of the problem (p. 35).

To test for this transitional phenomenon, Zutell employed five conservation tasks (one each for number, continuous quantity, mass, weight, and volume), two class inclusion tasks, and a picture integration task designed by David Elkind (1974). Each of these seven tasks and the procedures by which they are administered and scored have enjoyed rigorous empirical study and have moreover been found to correlate significantly with reading achievement as variously assessed (Almy 1966; Heatherly 1972; Elkind 1974, for example). It was Zutell's expectation that a better understanding of this relationship might be gained by assessing the correlations between these varied tasks and the more detailed sequences of word knowledge as reflected in our earlier studies.

For this comparison Zutell selected the long and short vowel categories studied by Beers but limited exemplar words to the lower frequency level, as these had proved the more sensitive in the earlier work. To these he added exemplars testing for knowledge of long markers (the *ed* suffix) and consonant doubling and open syllable (*bat, batting; rake, raking*). In addition he included an exemplar for vowel extension, as seen in words like *compete-competition*, where the reduced vowel in the second may be "known" from its long form in the root. These were composed into two eighteen-word spelling lists which were administered in May to all children in grades one through four of an elementary school in Culpepper, Virginia. After eliminating those subjects whose spelling attempts were nonexistent or random, fifteen children per grade were selected by lot from the remainder and on the following day given seven decentration tasks.

The ratings of long and short vowel spellings were essentially like those of Beers, but with these emendations. Because only children who would attempt spellings were included in the sample, a zero rating was given to those attempts that fell outside of one of the predicted categories. Thus, a spelling of SCUD for *skid* would be so rated since this substitution does not meet the criteria of letter-name or transitional vowel substitution. In addition, Zutell expanded the upper end of the scale to include correct target elements in an otherwise incorrectly spelled word, e.g., SCID for *skid*. This rating fell between that for transitional and fully correct spelling. Examples of the scoring criteria for long markers, consonant doubling, and vowel extension appear in Table 1.

These different error categories were, as expected, managed differently across the four grades. The long-short vowel transitions were largely accomplished by grade three. Tense markers and consonant doubling were of medium difficulty, while vowel extension was clearly not fully accomplished by the fourth grade. Canonical correlations, with grade controlled, showed a significant relationship be-

Table 1. Scoring Criteria for Invented Spellings across Five Target Categories

Category	Strategy	Score	Examples
Short Vowel	unclassifiable	0	krof (*craft*) scod (*skid*)
	vowel omitted	1	krft, scd
	closest long vowel	2	crift, sced
	transitional	3	creft, scad
	vowel correct, incorrect form	4	kraf, scid
	correct form	5	craft, skid
Long Vowel	unclassifiable	0	crop (*creep*), slom (*slime*)
	letter name	1	crep, slim
	transitional	2	crip, slam
	vowel correct, marking incorrect	3	creyp, sliym
	vowel correctly marked, incorrect form	4	creap, sime
	correct form	5	creep, slime
Long Marker	unclassifiable	0	rake (*raked*), cet (*cheated*)
	letter name	1	rakt, chetd
	d marker	2	rakd, cheatd
	vowel (not *e*, not *o*, + *d*)	3	racid, cheatud
	marker correct, incorrect form	4	raced, cheeted
	correct form	5	raced, cheated
Consonant Doubling	unclassifiable	0	flop (*flopped*), wad (*wading*)
	letter name	1	flpt, wadn
	short, undoubled	2	floped
	long, doubled	3	wadding
	doubling correct, incorrect form	4	flapped, weding
	doubling correct, correct form	5	flopped, wading

Table 1. (con't)

Category	Strategy	Score	Examples
Vowel Extension	unclassifiable	0	xpln (*explain*) = xplntn (*explanation*)
	letter name	1	xplan-explnashon
	vowel present, unextended	2	explain-explashon
	vowel incorrectly extended	3	explain-explaination
	vowel correctly extended, incorrect form	4	explain-xplanashon
	correct form	5	explain-explanation

tween the decentration measures and spelling. Conservation tables contributed most to the short vowel category, and the picture categorization task contributed most to the vowel extension category. Zutell's summary of these results:

> An analysis of variance of the 30 spelling scores of the 60 subjects revealed that there were significant main effects for grade and spelling category, as well as a significant interaction between grade and category. There was a general increase in scores as grade level increased, though the total of category mean scores were unexpectedly lower for grade one than for grade two. The mean scores for grades one and two were substantially lower than the mean scores for grades three and four across all categories, though there was also a large difference in mean scores between grades three and four for B_5, the Vowel Extension category. There was also a general decrease in scores for each grade as the level of spelling category increased. A ceiling effect was noted for grades three and four on the first three categories, while grades one and two did poorly on the last three categories, with B_5 being slightly more difficult.
>
> A canonical correlation was obtained (r = .67, p < .01) linking the sets of decentration and spelling variables. A factor analysis indicated that there were two distinct factors, one for the decentration tasks and one for the spelling categories. These factors were themselves highly correlated (r = .56, p < .01). A second factor analysis, in which the effects of grade level on the intercorrelations was controlled, produced the same general patterns as the first factor analysis, though the

amount of variance accounted for was somewhat reduced. The two factors remained quite distinct and correlated ($r = .36$, $p < .01$).

Several specific intercorrelations were noted. Continuous Quantity was the decentration task most highly correlated with the spelling categories, maintaining a .01 level of significance with each spelling category, even after grade level had been controlled. The Short Vowel Category was the spelling variable most highly correlated with the decentration tasks, especially with Mass, Weight, and Continuous Quantity, retaining a .01 level of significance for the correlations with each of these even after grade level was controlled. Finally, the correlations between the *Picture Integration Test and Vowel Extension* was also significant at the .01 level in both factor analyses (pp. 74–75).

Despite the fact that the progression both in spelling and decentration scores was somewhat flawed by the unexpectedly low performance of the second grade sample, it does, nonetheless, appear that the advance in spelling competence is both cognitive and developmental in nature. Thus while the use of "letter-name strategy" decreased across grades, it was employed even in grade three (seventeen occurrences). Further, in the consonant doubling task, while there was again incorrect response between grades three and four, a significant incidence of overgeneralization was found at both levels, as in the spelling of WADDING for *wading*.

The separation of the spelling and decentration tasks factorially supports a belief in the basic difference between those two kinds of performances. The strength of the correlation between them, however (which was maintained when grade, or years of experience, was controlled), gives support to the belief that some common developmental cognitive competencies must underlie achievement on both tasks.

The pedagogical implications of these findings are, I think, these: To the degree that an advancing phonological knowledge demands operations like those assumed to underlie the Piagetian tasks here used, one may expect fairly wide individual differences among children in their rate of advancement in the formulation of such knowledge. Moreover, one must expect that such delays will not answer to the direct teaching of these relationships. Efforts to teach conservation tasks have been notoriously unsuccessful. Further, to the degree that a preoperational state of word knowledge provides the learner with less conceptual control of words, the acquisition of words into the "sight vocabulary" and their correct production in spelling must place increasingly heavy demands on memory. If, in such a circumstance, sufficient stress is experienced by the learner, one would predict a decrease in exploration and a tendency to fixate on primitive and superficial strategies for learning.

It must follow from this view of advancing word knowledge that instructional programs, which march at standard rates of word and "skill" introduction, do so at considerable hazard to large numbers of children. It would seem that programs should be adopted in which children have a rich and extended opportunity to explore words and to treat them as they best can—with no greater volume of words than they can comfortably maintain.

Higher Order Phonological Knowledge

We were interested next to see whether or not we could examine more closely the vowel extension category which appeared to be entering the repertoire of fourth grade spellers. This project was undertaken by S. Templeton (1976). Limiting his sample to able spellers drawn from grades six, eight, and ten, he added stress and vowel reduction or shift to the dependent variable, correct spelling. His design made it possible to look at phonological knowledge cross-sectionally and to do so both in relation to spelling and as a function of different information sources surrounding the base word, i.e., isolated versus contextual and oral versus visual presentations. By this means, Templeton examined the relatively advanced "higher order" phonological knowledge implied by Chomsky and Halle as obtaining for words of Romance derivation. The specific patterns are those in words like *divine-divinity* where addition of the formative *ity* yields no change in stress but a vowel shift from long to short, and in words like *compete-competition* where the addition of the formative *ition* yields a change in stress and a reduction of the previously stressed vowel to schwa.

To test for these effects, Templeton composed a twenty-four word list containing both real and legal pseudo-words (Tables 2 and 3). These were presented to subjects so that for each type they might either hear the base word spoken or see it in printed form. In addition they were either given a sentence in which the derived form would fit, or they were asked to speak the derived form without this cue. The subjects' spoken responses were tape-recorded, and then they were then asked to spell the word.

Ratings for stress were 1 for correct primary stress and 0 for no response or incorrect stress. For vowel alternation, a score of 1 was applied to a correct vowel shift or reduction (including in this condition a correct short vowel of markedly shortened quality) and 0 if no attempt was made or if the vowel was characterized by incorrect quantity or quality. To obtain a score of 1 for spelling it was necessary to meet three conditions: correct representation of the vowel element in the derived form, deletion or change of the final consonant of the base, and a correct representation of the suffix. Thus, it was possible to spell the vowel element correctly yet receive a score of 0 if the final consonants were not appropriately changed. Templeton's spelling assessment was, in this regard, somewhat less finely grained than that employed by Zutell. A five-way analysis of variance was applied to

Table 2. Base Words Presented in Isolation

Spelling	Pronunciation	Suffix	Word + Suffix Pronunciation
tropane	/tropeyn/	ity	/tropænlti/
deprave	/dəpreyv/	tity	/dəprævlti/
pletaim	/plɛteym/	ation	/plɛtəmeyšən/
defame	/dəfeym/	ation	/dɛfəmeyšən/
ostrite	/ostrayt/	tion	/ostrlšən/
contrite	/kəntrayt/	tion	/kəntrlǎən/
tonfide	/tʌnfayd/	ence	/tonfldɛna/
define	/dəfayn/	ition	/defənlšən/
percose	/pɝkous/	ity	/pɛrkəslti/
osmosis	/osmousls/	ic	/ozmotlk/
renote	/rənout/	ation	/rɛnəteyšən/
console	/kənsoul/	ation	/kənsəleyšən/

Table 3. Base Words with Contextual Facilitation

Spelling	Pronunciation	Suffix	Word + Suffix Pronunciation
retrave (The_____that John used impressed us.)	/rətreyv/	ity	/rətrævlti/
urbane (George's_____impressed all of us.)	/ɝbeyn/	ity	/ɝbænlti/
osplain (We watched the_____for a long time.)	/ospleyn/	ation	/ospləneyšən/
exclaim (Patty's_____told us she was happy.)	/ɛkskleym/	ation	/ɛkskləmeyšən/
tivine (This_____is confusing.	/təvayn/	ity	/təvlnlti/
describe (Bert gave us a good_____of the thief.)	/dɛskrayb/	tion	/dɛskrlpšən/
ospire (We all enjoyed the_____.)	/ospayɝr/	ation	/ospəreyšən/
derive (I know the_____of that.)	/dərayv/	ation	/dɝrəveyšən/

these data, and the three dependent measures were intercorrelated.

Findings for stress and vowel alternation showed significant gains between grade six and the two higher grades, which did not themselves differ. For spelling, there were no differences across grades. Visual presentation, that is seeing the base word in print rather than simply hearing it spoken, made a significant difference in correctness of vowel alternations and stress assignment. The presence of context influenced all three variables, correctness of stress, vowel alternation, and spelling. Whether a word was a real English word or not had little influence upon correctness of spelling, but real words were spoken more correctly in the derived form than were the legal pseudo-words.

Intercorrelation showed significant relationships between vowel alternation and stress assignment and spelling at all three grade levels. At grade ten, vowel alternation also was significantly related to spelling. The correlations between spelling and the other two variables were relatively low in grades six and eight (.20–.52) and reasonably strong at grade ten (.70–.77).

In general, these findings were in the direction predicted by Templeton and would appear to support the belief that higher order phonological knowledge is related to experience with written language and attained late rather than early in the school years. It had been predicted that spelling scores too would differ across grades. That they did not is interesting. Subjects, of course, had been chosen on the basis of their teachers' assertion that they were good spellers. Further, they all attained a score of seventy-five percent or better on a fairly demanding informal spelling pre-test. Thus, on a *power* dimension it may be that the three groups were relatively comparable despite their differences in age and experience. If this is the case, then the corresponding gains in higher order phonological knowledge (stress and vowel alternation scores) and the rising correlation of these with correctness in spelling may be thought of as a gain in quality of spelling competence. Intuitively this interpretation makes sense. Furthermore, it accords with Chomsky's speculations about the matter, as well as those of Moskowitz (1973) who concluded that higher order phonological knowledge must derive from experience with written language and from a fairly advanced and abstract segment of that language.

It is also interesting to consider the influence of the condition of presentation on correctness in spelling. The availability of context makes it more likely that Romance-derived words such as these will be both spoken and spelled correctly. Of this finding Templeton wrote the following:

> For years many teachers of reading, for example, have encouraged students to first read to the end of the sentence if they cannot identify a word (Smith 1971). This strategy is supposed to provide information on several fronts, the semantic, the syntactic, and the orthographic. A preoccupation with trying to identify the word by first breaking it into syllables, sounding out beginning consonants or consonant clusters, proceeding to the vowel element(s) and so on, is held to seriously constrain the amount of information available to the reader. Phonological implications or morphophonemics, and more recently, transformational generative grammar, challenge the efficacy of dealing with words

in isolation. Information from beyond the word boundary very often appears necessary (p. 101).

Templeton's findings tend to reinforce my belief that there is a complex conceptual structure underlying the word knowledge of the mature speaker/reader and that this knowledge derives in important part from an extended experience with written language. One may see in this circumstance, moreover, the roots of a pedagogical dilemma. To know how to spell, one must know many words, but to know many words, one must know how to spell. Some years ago Smith (1971) came to a very similar conclusion regarding the plight of beginning readers. Wanting sufficient word knowledge to identify meaningful chunks of print, they are denied access to those syntactic and semantic resources that make possible the wider apprehension of the fluent reader. Here indeed is a state of affairs well suited to inspire methodological wars. The child must learn about words or he will never learn to read; the child must learn to read or he'll never learn about words. The history of reading instruction lends support to this view.

Smith made two deceptively simple, but, in my opinion, eminently just recommendations for instruction. He advised first that teachers be helpful—that they find and employ every reasonable means to make reading easy. Second, he cautioned that children should be protected against an overdependence on and belief in those mediational tactics—sounding out words, for example—that are but a temporary aid or bridge to the altogether different process of reading employed by the mature reader.

It seems to me that similar conclusions may apply to the somewhat narrower field of word knowledge. As Read (1975) and Gibson and Levin (1975) have shown, children bring a remarkable body of knowledge to their initial attempts at word formation. To augment that knowledge, they must exercise their ideas and test them against what is given. They must have an opportunity to make errors in word construction, and they must have access to standard spelling, not only in the eye but in the mind. Pedagogically the trick will be to keep these modes in balance—the disposition to construct in certain ways and the knowledge of "what is right." There must be a play-off between quality of knowledge and power, and this should be maintained, I think not simply in grade one but throughout life.

Classroom Influences and the Effects of Dialect

Our studies of children's knowledge of words are now continuing in a variety of directions and are in varying states of completion. It should be recognized, I think, that our work has been the work of beginners in a new and complex field. I would warn all from a false belief that we have proceeded without blunders or that we have found truth and final answers, for we have not. I do, on the other hand, have a profound confidence in the work carried through by Charles Read (1975), and I take comfort that our findings have marched with his as we have explored for these phenomena in primary classrooms and upward through the grades. That letter-name and transitional strategies occur regardless of instructional method has been recently reconfirmed by Beers *et al.* (1977) in an analysis of spelling responses from a random sampling of classrooms in the Detroit area. Further, the correlation between this progression of spelling competence and achievement in Piagetian tasks (Goldschmid and Bentler 1968) was found for a second time by Carol Beers (1976) in a study also conducted in the Detroit area. Finally, there is some evidence that the spelling decisions that children make do not differ across dialect boundaries (Stever 1976).

In this latter study, Stever applied a set of low frequency word exemplars for long and short vowels *a*, *e*, and *i* to a sample of second graders over a six-month period. Each word to be spelled was elicited from a picture and verbal cues by the examiner. For example, "Here is a picture of something you might wear around your neck. What are these? (*Beads*) That is right. Now spell the word."

The children's pronunciations for each word were tape-recorded and then transcribed phonetically. From this pool, groups (n = 12) were formed to meet the criteria of high and low socioeconomic status and standard and nonstandard dialect. Thereafter, at one month intervals, the same words, but in random order, were cued by picture alone for spelling. These were then rated on a scale similar to those employed by Beers (1974) and Zutell (1975) but always on the basis of the child's initial pronunciation of the word. Thus, the child who pronounced *stick* /stɪk/ (rhymes with peek) is presumed to have reached the initial spelling STEK for reasons which are different from those of the child pronouncing it in the standard form. With dialect controlled, no differences were found between standard and nonstandard speakers. Nor were any main effects found for socioeconomic class, though the lower group began lower and evidenced more positive progress. It is fairly clear that a ceiling effect obscured differences here since the upper group had a preponderance of "correct response" in the latter trials.

That dialect should not, in and of itself, interfere with learning to spell would seem quite probable in terms of phonological theory. As discussed earlier, the written and base lexical forms of the word are reasoned to be similar and relatively stable, allowing for wider range of surface variation in an ordered and predictable manner. Children must adjust their own spoken language in their own way to a standard form which is common to the larger language community. To the degree that this is so, it would seem to me to follow that an opportunity to construct words in one's own way and adjust these to the more abstract "correct forms" would be equally necessary for standard and nonstandard speakers.

As I look back over this ten-year study period, I have the feeling that we have indeed made progress. Initially there were hunches and, for my part at least, an incredible feeling of excitement that we might come to grips with that demon "English Spelling." I believe that we have done so, and though we find him a wonderfully complex creature—far too intricate to map in some scope and sequence chart for pupils to learn—I believe that he is demon no more. Instead, the written English word appears to be a form toward which children will tend in very natural ways as they apply their language to worthy purposes.

Stages of Word Knowledge

At this point it may be appropriate to summarize our findings in a rough progressive schedule. It is in this way that we have come to use them informally as we diagnose and teach. We are presently studying data from a carefully prepared spelling inventory from which we will derive quite specific statements about spelling concepts as they relate to power and experience. For now, however, I will give an informal description of the sequence.

To begin with, it is helpful to recall that children begin to learn about words long before they come to school. At a very early age they will make marks with a pencil if they are given one, and their handiwork will look somewhat like the drawing in the margin, a wholly uninterpretable graphic (Gibson and Levin 1975). By degrees they gain more control of matters and are seen to move their pencils with intention until at last crude pictures are formed. Then, a most remarkable thing often happens. The child will handle his pencil altogether differently from the way that he did in drawing. Somewhere near his picture he will make some forms like this those at right. If you ask him what he is doing he will tell you that he is writing!

It is now that the child is likely to begin to ask what letters are and, more particularly, the letters to write his name. Soon his graphic creations will look like that in the margin, which is a rendition of my first name and probably much neater than my own first efforts. Nonetheless, it illustrates the want of line and orientation that regularly characterizes such early attempts. Many children at this stage continue to scribble and to mix letters and symbols in a variety of inventive ways. Gentry (1977) has labeled those creations "Preliterate, prephonetic."

The next thing that happens, particularly in a school setting, is really quite remarkable. If you ask the child how to write a word, he will put down the initial consonant and stop with that. Thus *dog* is D, *cat* is K, and *dress* very often is JR. It is as if the child were still uncertain about what a word is but knows at least what it isn't *and* refuses now to use any nonallowable symbols. Moreover, it is also clear that the child at this stage has the idea of letter name in relation to sound. He is able to capture the beginning, but thereafter the word object slips from his grasp. We call this stage "Preliterate, phonetic."

Once children know their letters and are beginning to read, their construction of words takes on a complex and consistent form. Not surprisingly they spell correctly those words that they "remember." Most other words that they chose to write, however, tend to appear in a form we have termed spelling by "letter name." Each phoneme is rendered by the letter whose name denotes that sound element or that is, in the child's judgment, closest to that sound element. Thus, they might write "The rain in Spain stayed mainly on the plain," thus: THE RAN EN SPAN STAD MANLE ON THE PLAN. For the short vowels, of course, there is no letter name. To render these, children employ their own independent judgment in the matter and do so with remarkable consistency. They might write the sentence, "We had a pet fish that got under a rock," as: WE HAD A PAT FES THAT GIT ONDR A RIK. Although children come to these decisions for quite abstract and tacit reasons, it is quite easy for literate adults to remember what they will do. *A* substitutes for short *e*, *E* for short *i*, *I* for short *o*, *O* for short *u*, and *U* not surprisingly for the double *o* in *moon*. I am grateful to Gentry for pointing out this vocalic aid to memory.

There is, of course, a great deal more to this letter-name strategy than is shown in these illustrations. The details of this stage have already been presented (pp. 51–56). The important point for the present is to see that beginning readers not only memorize words but they also employ a complex strategy of orthography that is consistent and incredibly accurate phonetically. In a very important sense, this whole array of "errors" in spelling is natural, developmentally normal, and, in this sense, correct and healthy.

A second very important point should be understood about the "letter-name" stage. To achieve this level of performance, children must have attained a stable concept of word as a bound examinable figure. This concept of word phenomenon has been carefully described by Morris (1980). His work helps to explain the difficulty, indeed the folly, of attempting to teach auditory discrimination for word elements prior to the establishment of this basic concept.

In due time children's strategy for short vowel substitution is defirmed and abandoned. Despite the fact that their inner "hunch" would render *fish* as FES, the data from their growing sight vocabulary declare that things are otherwise, and they accept it. At this stage they might write WE HAD A PET FISH THAT GOT UNDR A ROKE. At this same time they begin to change their long vowel constructions. Thus our first sentence might now begin to look like this: THE RANE IN SPAEN STAID MAINLE ON THE PLEAN. Errors of this kind seem to reflect a sense of the marking system for long vowels, though the particular patterns for each are not yet sorted out. We have labeled this stage "Vowel transition."

With the advent of this transitional stage, which often occurs toward the end of the first grade year, children's ability to extend their reading vocabulary increases dramatically. Usually another full year is required, however, before the long vowel patterns stabilize. In addition, there are evident gaps in these children's "knowledge" of the significance of spelling patterns in inflected forms. Thus, as "The rain in Spain" comes to be spelled correctly, the inflected forms *raining* and *shining* and *smaller* and *fatter* may often appear as RAINNING, SHINNING, SMALER, and FATER. Interestingly, too, the word *sail* might be spelled SAIL while *sailor* is rendered SALOR.

Once again it is important to understand that errors in spelling are to be expected as children advance *toward* that standard which is suitable for adults. Further, I believe it to be a serious mistake to convey to children by word or deed that this standard is arbitrary and hopelessly hard to reach. The standard patterns into which single syllable words typically fall are limited and *can* be learned. Homonyns, far from being difficult, are useful hallmarks to be learned and enjoyed.

When basic vowel patterns are reasonably well in hand, *then* children can begin to learn the principle of consonant doubling as it marches with open and closed syllables in longer words. Armed with this knowledge they then have the means to examine polysyllabic words and make use of them. Tragically, these simple guides are almost never adequately demonstrated for children nor are they given anywhere near the needed practice in *using* this knowledge to study words.

The ability to examine a word logically is required if children are to assess the lower frequency vocabulary of the middle school years. If a solid foundation is built, then we may expect children to master, over time, a great number of regularizing conditions that otherwise must appear as wild confusion. Consider some of these related words: *persuade-persuasion, act-action, finance-financial, unit-united, vision-visible, port-portable*. It is words of this kind, and many others, that yield predictable and interesting errors during the late school years. Most will yield to analysis, if relatively simple basic skills are applied and a good dictionary consulted by pupils *and their teachers!*

The Advent of Reading and Writing

5

Understanding Reading

The key to an understanding of how one learns to read and write is to recognize the distinction between tacit and surface knowledge. The former is real. It is the basic stuff of which knowing is composed, yet it is complex, abstract, and unspecifiable either from without or from within. Surface knowledge, on the other hand, is mythic, unreal, and incomplete. It is an approximation of, a metaphorical assertion about true knowledge; however, in this form it is concrete, measurable, and specific. Our learning of language and our interfacing this language with graphics is an unfolding of tacit knowledge. What we may say about this competence and its gradual realization by a learner is severely limited. The reality of reading and writing lies in our doing so, yet the steps by which we march toward this competence are ever less reliable, more arbitrary, and less true as they are specified concretely.

Consider, for example, the learning of a letter. I may say to a child this is the letter named "A," and it is formed with a pencil in a certain way. This statement is true as far as it goes, but it is deceptively incomplete. It omits altogether the question of what a letter *is* and what the learner must learn to know that letter in relation to its spoken name and its occurrence in written words. Now, we may conceive, as Gibson and Levin (1975) do, that the underlying stuff of letters is a set of contrastive features and that it is a tacit sensitivity to these that underlies the possibility of discriminant letter identification. In taking this step, however, we have moved to the level of tacit knowledge and the statement of an abstraction. If we attempt to name those features of the letter—calling them diagonality, intersection, symmetry and the like, we speak of concrete truth which begs the question of what the nature of such features really are both in the world and in the mind. For example, it is helpful to know that neurologists can identify in the brain of a frog a node in the visual track that fires uniquely in the presence of small moving objects (Smith 1971). Such a finding supports the metaphor of feature theory, but it most certainly does not help specify in concrete detail the complexity of letter identification. The only solid ground that we may find in this matter is to understand that man *can* identify letters and that our descriptions of how he does so are incomplete.

Reading and learning to read are quite beyond the reach of science, and I believe that they will always be so. Reading may be learned only in the doing of it, and any direction in the process that we offer will always be distinct from the process itself, useful only if used, but false and wholly useless alone or as a series of commands to be remembered or executed. Thus it is that reading skills must be understood. While they are concrete and while they can be measured, they are incomplete, metaphorical rather than true, and arbitrary both in number and in form.

The distinction here made between tacit and surface knowledge has very deep philosophical roots. It rests, indeed, in the central argument of the Meno where Socrates grapples with the dilemma of human knowledge and concludes that in essence it is from within rather than without. Aristotle differed on this point and so has the scientific tradition that followed him. Science has built its theories in response to the measurable units of surface events. Nonetheless, the dilemma remains. While scientists may reject the Platonic concept of soul, they can approach truth only through abstractions that are held by faith to be ultimately knowable in a concrete sense. These constructs, however, are different altogether from those surface events now measured and manipulated. The paradigmatic shift in the philosophy of science (see Kuhn 1970, for example) represents a reawakening to the primacy of such abstract formulations for the conceptualization and study of human learning. The effect of this changed view upon pedagogy will certainly yield renewed sensitivity on our part to the distinction between what is learned and what is taught, between skillfulness and skill, between tacit and surface knowledge. In no field, I believe, will this change prove more helpful than in the study of language, reading, and writing where the mythic character of surface events has so long deceived us.

Arcane though these matters may seem, and in fact are, there is really no mystery about them at all. That is, the phenomenon of tacit knowledge is a common sensical and familiar thing that we can easily know and respond to. An example may clarify this point.

It happens that a few years ago I undertook to learn to ride a hunter in the English style, which was a fairly demanding enterprise for one who was both middle-aged and wholly unfamiliar with horses. It has provided me, however, with an opportunity both to learn something new and to observe the course of that learning as I did so. The experience has been surprisingly informative.

My instructor proceeded thus. She lodged me in the rough approximation of a correct position in the saddle on a gentle and willing horse. Then I worked with a small group of other beginners at slow gaits in a ring. This was alternated with easy cross-country treks and punctuated now and then with a safe "hilltop" view of the hunt. She told us almost nothing about how to ride at first, other than to say vaguely that it was somewhat like dancing. In the rare event that one of us did something right, she was quick to note it. Errors were cor-

The Advent of Reading and Writing **5**

rected largely after the fact, very casually and only when she judged that the corrective measure could be heeded. Thus we learned to ride by riding, under the direction of a teacher who staged the setting so that we could do so, painfully and awkwardly, perhaps, but without risk to life and limb. It was made absolutely clear that we should attend regularly and concentrate on the task. Yet the early boredom of work in a dusty ring was abundantly relieved by cross-country rambles and hill-top views. I believe her strategy to have been brilliant and a well-nigh perfect example of how we should teach children to read.

I must confess, however, that at the time I found the absence of a full set of directions about how to do it strangely disturbing. In due course I bought the best text on horsemanship I could find and read it cover to cover. A surprise awaited me. Though I understood what I had read, I could not exercise a hundredth part of it on the back of a horse. Consider this, for example. If you wish to know on which diagonal you are trotting, you simply note which foreleg is forward as you lift or post in the saddle. Skillful riders can tell without looking, but a beginner cannot tell for looking. By the time his mind has walked through the relationships to be made, the thing to be noted is gone. It is not until the mind and the body can trot with the horse that a glance can record the event. It is this that we know as tacit knowledge. A symphony of coordinate perceptual data centrally housed underpins the acquisition of each "skill," and it is knowledge the details of which we are quite unable to name and number either in the brain or in the world.

When the body/mind knows what it must, the skill is taken at a stroke and thence with practice automated into the repertoire of the rider. Note further that the skill itself is quite arbitrary and conventional. One might ride to town and back, flying fences all the way, without the conscious knowledge of diagonals. The same is true for seat position and a myriad of signals by hand and leg and weight. Yet one could not make such a ride without having ridden and learned those tacit things the mind must know in order to see and execute its will by these arbitrary sets of surface means.

One could not possibly learn to ride by practicing leg positions on a hobbyhorse. Nor, I submit, has anyone ever learned to read by the practice of such hobbyhorse skills. The long-enduring argument in reading pedagogy as to which set of skills is best is simply bogus. The possible combination of such skills is well-nigh infinite. What serves is fine; what does not is dross. They have meaning only in the context of the act and are but surface markers of inner complex knowledge. One learns to read and write by reading and writing, by exercising the will to understand and to communicate.

The language beginner requires both skill and example, and for learning the spoken language, society seems to provide these conditions naturally. For learning the written language, however, at least for most of us, teachers are needed too. Their job, however, cannot be to build language into the child. Instead, they must support and exercise its use, judge the learner's growing competence, and supply those conventional suggestions when and as they will serve.

As we have seen, the pedagogy of reading has tended to disintegrate over the past century into a patterning of skills in scope and sequence and the measuring of competence by means of the standardized test. In following this direction we have increasingly neglected the act of reading and writing and the context of sociocultural forces that support such action. We have neglected as well our responsibility to judge the developing competence of learners.

I am satisfied that the recent change of perspective taken by the human sciences has made it possible for us to recover this lost ground. The work of my students and myself has derived from such new models, and from this work we have been able to identify far more clearly the dimensions of that tacit knowledge which underlies English spelling. The consequence of such developing states of knowledge may be observed in the characteristic spellings children compose in the natural act of writing. By observing children's writing, teachers may judge the students' developing competence in word knowledge. And do note that I use the word *judge* not *test*, for this is not a testable matter but one for qualitative judgment.

Our work is a small, but I think important part of a rich outpouring of research and observation that does support teacher judgment in this sense. In the following sections I will try to sketch in some of the benchmarks that reflect the evolution of this tacit knowledge of written language. This will be divided into four stages: (1) that period before formal reading commences, i.e., reading readiness, (2) the delicate period of beginning reading, (3) early reading, and (4) the long progression toward reading maturity.

Readiness for Learning to Read

Before a child has much chance of learning to read on his own or of responding successfully to beginning reading instruction, there are a great many things that he must have learned about language, the world, and himself and his role in that world. Moreover, his home, community, and culture, too, must meet certain very important criteria if literacy is to be attained with naturalness and ease. Finally, reasonable physical health and a command of the spoken language are important as well, and it is with these latter that I will begin.

☐ Language, Health, and Intelligence

When children are born, they are fitted, neurologically, to acquire their mother tongue during the first four to five years of life. This phenomenon is universal and occurs over wide ranges of intelligence and cultural prosperity. Doubtless, physical well-being and a gifted mind are felicitious for language learning, just as there must be levels of deprivation and intellectual want that might prevent it altogether.

Nonetheless, the range is very great. Many, many children in the most wretched circumstances learn their own language well. Thus, failure of spoken language to occur, within reasonable and sound limits, must be considered a signal of some possible physical impairment and does merit prompt medical referral. On the other hand, the presence of language in a child may be taken as a prerequisite for learning to read and as one major piece of evidence of readiness for doing so.

In general, children of lower intelligence tend to acquire language at a somewhat slower pace than others, as they do also master more slowly and less fully other aspects of knowledge of the world. Therefore, it is probable that in most such cases readiness for reading will occur later rather than earlier. It is simply true that some children are speaking fluently at age three and a half and four while others may not do so until six and a half or seven. Some may therefore learn to read early, others much later. If this difference in pace is honored, however, both may learn to read.

Intelligence, per se, is simply not very important for learning to read, or put differently, learning to read apparently makes but modest demands on intelligence. A simple and, to me, very heart-warming example may help bring this point home.

Some years ago a seventeen-year-old young lady was brought to our Delaware Reading Center by her parents. She was beautifully groomed, well-mannered, composed, and also, though less obviously so, intellectually dull. She had had, through her parents' fine management, every proper advantage. They now wished that she might continue with us the beginning she had made in recent years toward learning to read. We accepted her gladly and learned much from her achievement, for she did learn to read and read well, at her own intellectual level. I can recall that she at age 19 and my daughter at age 9 were equally charmed by the stories of Laura Ingalls Wilder. Ultimately, this young girl became a librarian's helper in an elementary school, where her gentle ways and love of children's stories were an inspiration to young and old alike.

Such was the reading accomplishment of a person whom doctors at two of the top medical centers in this country had categorized as a borderline mental defective—verbal I.Q. 70. Given the requisite advantages and time, what might we do for people in the 85 to 100 I.Q. range? Yet these are the people who fill our institutions, and who also cannot read.

Barring a specific language disability, a topic I will consider more fully in the final chapter, matters of health, nourishment, energy and the like would appear to be in an indirect, though nonetheless important, relationship to reading readiness and learning to read. As a rule of thumb I think one may say that where the opportunity to explore the world is restricted, learning will be similarly restricted. Thus, a good breakfast may not prepare children to read, but it may well provide the pep they need to learn what they must before being able to do so. Any nation committed to literacy must have a sharp concern for those harsh conditions of poverty which necessarily will restrict the quest for knowledge.

In a similar vein, emotional adjustment too will play a part in learning. Knowledge in its essence must derive from the will to understand, to doubt, to test, to reason and resolve. And so, in a very real sense, its advancement will depend on a certain degree of self-reliance and a disposition to cope. I am impressed in this regard by the work of B. L. White and J. C. Watts (1973) who have found a strong correlation between this dimension of adjustment and academic success. Initially, the newborn is quite helpless. He must learn of trust from those who nurture him, and only from such trust may he thence learn to trust himself. I believe that parents can do no more helpful thing for their children than maintain their contract of helping where help is required and of requiring children to do for themselves those things they are able to do.

☐ The Cultural Imperative

A critical area of learning in the early years has to do with experiences with written language. There are many facets of this topic and all, I think, have a major influence on when a child will learn to read. The sociocultural aspect of this influence is perhaps best illustrated by Marie Clay (1976) in her descriptive comparison of Maori, Melanesian, and Caucasian children in New Zealand. Despite the fact that the Melanesians were of a relatively poorer class, minority "foreign" group, they achieved quite as well as the whites. The Maori children (who were also poor) in contrast made very little progress in grade one. While most did eventually learn to read, their progress was both later occurring and slower.

Clay's analysis of the distinction between the Maori and Melanesians is informative. The Maori, it appears, is a dying culture. The language is disappearing and with it the oral literature, customs, and beliefs. There is a distinct lack of cohesion and community purpose. For the Melanesians, this is not so. They are a cohesive, socially vigorous group who maintain communication with their home islands by letter, and they are much given to church-going and Sunday School. Written language is thus a vital part of the Melanesian child's experience, and he is exposed to it abundantly and meaningfully.

I am inclined to think that it may be taken as a premise that where folk tale and written language lack significance for a culture, its children will find it difficult to respond to even the best instruction. This most certainly does not mean that they cannot learn to read. The evidence is clear that they can, but that learning will occur later—after a reasonable exposure to graphics and to the realization of the office that writing serves. Pedagogically, the implications are twofold. First, the teacher of such children must have the kind of patience that is born of understanding, not that of the clinched fist held back. Second, concrete steps must be taken to immerse these children in a written language that makes a difference in their lives. The universal truths exemplified in children's literature, presented orally, of course, must reach them before they can be expected to reach out themselves to print. I do not think that this can be accomplished by video-tape. It will require a flesh and blood teacher who is wise, determined, optimistic, and responsive. Sylvia Ashton-Warner's classic account (1963) of teaching the Maori children is a case in point.

☐ Written Language—Its Cadence and Form

One of the things that we have known for years about reading is that the experience of having been read to abundantly as a child predicts success in grade one far more reliably than does intelligence. That this should be so is understandable not only on the grounds of the meaning and purpose of written language but also on the basis of its special syntatic structure. Children reared in a nonliterate environment learn only the grammar of the spoken language. They are naive about the special reference systems and organizational devices by which the written language compensates for the absence of eye contact, gesture, and stress. One could describe these differences technically, but I think it is not necessary here to do so.

Imagine yourself listening to a voice from behind a screen. First it is speaking; then it is reading from a text. Instantly you know which is which. You do so because the cadence and form of written English is part of your language knowledge. Only the most skillfully written and performed dialogue could fool you. Now try to imagine yourself approaching the reading of a text without such knowledge. What expectations could you have about the probable flow of context? Clearly it would be a most crippling state of affairs. This is the circumstance that confronts each child who has not experienced the pattern of written language before beginning to learn to read.

I think there are few who would not agree that being read to in a variety of settings and being told stories and hearing letters read and quotes from the newspaper (whether understood or not) are an incalculable advantage for the young child. But if this has been denied, what then? Here opinions differ. Some will argue that such a deficit in early experience will yield a life-time language disability. For my part, I believe that this is not so, provided that the necessary preparatory experiences are made available and failure and frustration avoided. Others argue that since the grammar and purpose of written language is not available to many beginners, it may be better to omit this aspect of the task and concentrate on letters and sounds and word forms in isolation. This does not seem sound at all to me because our studies suggest so clearly that word knowledge is intimately bound to meaning and syntax.

My own persuasion is that the best beginning that can be made, in addition to story-telling, reading aloud, role-playing and the like, is through the use of dictated experience stories. The activities that precede dictation are ideal for language modeling in a natural manner as one leads the youngster to examine and talk about some everyday experience—a basket of kittens, a bowl of fruit, the making of kites. The dictation by the child is a kind of test or language record, as he tells formally, gives an account of what he has observed and learned. The teacher writes down exactly what the child says, and he watches as she does so. Initially, dictation by inexperienced children will be single words and sentence fragments. Gradually, however, their productions change, and these records serve as a concrete witness to their gradual assimilation of the patterns of reporting and story-telling. Children seldom begin to remember words, as such, until their dictated accounts achieve a degree of structure and completeness. This experience with dictated stories, moreover, exposes these children to graphics about which they must learn a great deal before being ready to master a sight vocabulary and to read.

☐ Knowledge of Graphic Features

This brings me to the very important work of Eleanor Gibson and her associates (1975), which has begun to make clear the basic featural characteristics of writing systems and the means by which such graphic forms are able to convey visually so complex a phenomenon as language. In one of their studies it was shown that children as young as one and one half years evidenced interest and persistence in making scribbles when given a pencil and paper to write on. (The control group, given a stylus instead of a pencil, soon dropped it with indifference). And well they might. Consider, at age one and one half, the wonder, the magic of making lines appear!

Developmental studies of children's drawings demonstrate a progressive change in the kinds of contrastive graphs that are executed. Initially, the creation is an undifferentiated scribble. Then, one can identify the use of diagonals, intersection, closure, and the like. Thus, what graphics can be made to do appears to be a thing learned gradually and tacitly over these very early years. Such learning would appear to have a crucial importance for dealing with written language.

Writing, be it in English or Chinese, is very different in perspective from forests and trees and other things in three-dimensional space. It is also different from pictures and geometric figures on a page (Howes 1962). In feature theory (Smith 1971; also Gibson and Levin 1975) it is argued that letters are letters because they comprise a sufficient number of distinctive features to differentiate each from the other. Thus the letter A may be described as symmetry +, closure −, diagonality +, intersection +, circularity −, whereas the letter C would read symmetry −, closure −, diagonality −, intersection −, circularity +. It is reasoned that a full or partial readout of these distinctive features is what occurs along the visual pathways that connect the retinal image with the visual interpretation centers of the brain.

There does appear to be some neurological evidence of such feature-sensitive nodes (Smith 1971) and provided one does not treat the feature concept concretely and superficially, the theory appears to have considerable power. Specifically, concrete "features" like Chomsky's "base lexical entries" are profoundly abstract. We represent them by terms like diagonality and closure and the like, but they are not such specific entities in the global function of the brain. Thus one may not teach letter identification directly by teaching diagonality, closure, and orientation. The fact that such superficial perceptual training programs have been shown to have little relationship to reading achievement supports this position (Hammill *et al.* 1974; Hammill and Larsen 1974).

One may ask, of course, this question. If features are not "real," of what possible use is such a concept to educational theory and practice? The answer is that this theory is very valuable indeed. For one thing it explains why gross perceptual training is not germane to reading. Second, it suggests that experience with written language—letters, words, sentences—will be necessary on a fairly extended basis before actual letter and work identification can occur. Third, it suggests why it is that letters may not be taught or learned one at a time. The abstract meaning of letter is the feature system derived from all letters and thus quite undeducible from a single exemplar.

Lavine (as cited in Gibson and Levin 1975, pp. 233–39) has shown that children progressively learn to discriminate pictures from scribbles, scribbles from "writing" (Arabic, Chinese, English), and English writing from foreign writing at ages prior to learning to read. I have found that some prereading children can distinguish between some "legal" and "non-legal" English words, for example, tank versus NKTA. Herein lies powerful evidence, I think, of a rich primary conceptual grasp of the abstract structure of writing. This comes about, not through direct teaching, but from an exposure to written language in its natural uses and through an opportunity to experiment with writing tools. Lavine also found marked differences on these dimensions between advantaged and disadvantaged children. One cannot doubt the deleterious effect that want of this kind of experience must have on the beginning reading efforts of disadvantaged children.

Once the distinctive features of letters are grasped, the association of the name to each letter is a simple, almost automatic and inevitable thing. It is this knowledge that children bring to bear on words as they first begin to examine and invent them. Our Virginia studies of children's early writing are convincing on this point. There is still, however, one further dimension of written language knowledge that must precede this kind of production. Children must learn what words are.

☐ Concept of Word

How ridiculous, you may think. Certainly children know words; they use them all the time. Of course this is true, but to know words as individually analyzable units is a very different thing from knowing them tacitly in the production of oral language. To step outside of one's language and examine it as an object is a very high level intellectual task. Young children are largely quite unable to do so. One can see in this circumstance the familiar two-dimensional or relational thinking requirement characteristic of Piaget's concrete operational stage of cognitive development.

In a recent study by Papandropoulou and Sinclair (1974) children's responses to the question "What is a word?" are shown to follow a four-stage progression from the ages of four to ten years. Initially, children do not differentiate between the word and the object that it represents. Next, words are limited to objective referents, with the result that an article like *the* is omitted from the class. Only later at the six-to-eight year range do words stand as a bit of meaning independent of their referents—though meaning itself still lies not in the word unit but in the phrase or sentence. Not until these conceptualizations of word have been traversed do children treat words as independent meaning elements. In another recent empirical study, Downing and Oliver (1973–1974) found children confusing phonemes, syllables, and phrases with words when they were presented orally. And so indeed should we expect them to.

Many years ago, Stauffer pointed out to me and others that beginning readers do not at first identify words individually in their dictated story charts. Given the sentence, "My Daddy sails a big oyster boat," the beginner may be able to name the first and last words when they are pointed to but may still be quite unable to identify those in the middle, even though the full sentence is recalled and can be "read" word-for-word when the teacher points to the words in order. Indeed, I recall one bright beginner for whom even the last word posed a problem. When I pointed to the word *boat* and asked what word that was, he replied "*zero.*"

"How do you know?" I asked.

"Because my mother taught me," he crowed.

Letters and numbers he knew quite well, but word boundaries were not yet a part of his language knowledge. This would await further experience with written language, which I believe to be the necessary setting from which a concept of word derives. Moreover, it has long seemed to me potentially quite dangerous to condition children to "know" words before they have this concept of the bound figure with letters in it marching left to right. Otherwise, one cannot know what random set of features they may fasten on in conceptualizing words.

About how children learn the needed intial concept of word I am still somewhat uncertain; my speculation, however, is this. It seems very doubtful to me, particularly in the light of the Papandropoulou study (1974), that beginning readers are able to step back from and examine words objectively at the beginning. Further, I suspect that the eventual ability to do so, which as we have seen gradually emerges during the primary years, derives from experience with written language. It would be interesting to examine word knowledge among members of a nonliterate society. I think that there might well be some striking differences.

At all events, I feel confident that the initial grasp of the word unit is achieved by children tacitly. By slowing down the pace of "talk" and speaking to the print, the temporal-spatial match between spoken and written word is made, the significance of space and pause emerges, and the concept of word gradually crystallizes. Most early readers who learned without formal assistance cannot tell you how they did it, but in the vast majority of cases they did so by telling a well-known story to a book. One can see in this the tremendous advantage given the child who has been read aloud to abundantly. That more stately cadence of oral reading is already a part of his language and well suited to the eventual match with print. One can see this well, I think, in a partially negative example.

Consider this classic story opener. "Once upon a time there lived in a cottage by a forest a father and mother and their tiny baby." Imagining this read to a child, can you not hear the time spaces marching with the words—all except for *Onceuponatime*? If one examines children's early writing, one finds, not surprisingly, that they run this opener together in a variety of charming ways, even though they can differentiate each of the other words individually. From every angle it seems that being read to in the early years is of tremendous importance.

It is my opinion, also, that dictation by children is a sound way to introduce them to this word discovery process. Through it one may capitalize on the child's recall of what he said. In addition one has a graphic record of the child's general language development and so may know as it gradually takes the form of written English when to expect the miracle of reading to begin. Finally, these accounts provide a fully individualized language sample automatically adjusted to the purpose, meaning, and syntax of the child who dictates the account.

☐ Auditory Discrimination

Before leaving this topic, initial knowledge of word, one further point needs to be made. One of the best-known difficulties that beginning readers seem to have is discriminating the individual phonemic elements of words. This has led many educational theorists to advocate intensive auditory discrimination training in order to "teach young children their sounds" (Calfee 1972). Others have taken a quite different approach and advocated beginning with syllable units, somewhat after the manner used to teach Japanese children (Gibson and Levin 1975, p. 228). Gleitman and Rozin (1977) found, for example, that severely economically deprived and backward readers could learn quite readily by this syllable unit method, whereas they had failed utterly when required to deal with individual phonemic elements.

But there is a difficulty in all this. First of all, if children were not sensitive to the phonetic elements of speech, they could neither speak nor understand. Furthermore, it has been Read's finding (1975) and ours (Henderson and Beers 1980), as well as Noam and Carol Chomsky's (1970, 1976) that young children have not simply adequate phonetic discrimination abilities but unusually heightened facilities for such tasks. How is it then that they do so poorly on auditory discrimination exercises? I believe that the answer must lie in their prereading concept of word. With the term *kitty cat* being a sort of amorphous porridge of sounds and shapes, of fur and claws, meows and purrs, how would one expect a child to focus on the initial phonetic element /K/? They lack in their minds that bound figure that we call word, and thus they cannot give attention to it. When this concept is formed, however, we find them using their letter knowledge faultlessly as they work toward more and more abstract systems of spelling. They do so, moreover, whether or not letter sounds are "taught."

As noted under our "Stages of Word Knowledge" at the conclusion of chapter 4, a recent formal study of children's tacit concept of word (Morris 1980) has added substantial weight to the importance of this phenomenon. It appears quite clearly from this work that auditory discrimination for word elements, i.e., segmentation tasks, depend, for their execution, on a tacit knowledge of word. This is a state of affairs that we long thought to be true on the basis of clinical evidence. Morris's findings explain why auditory discrimination tasks are so difficult for many young children and so frustrating both for them and their teachers. Further, they show that the pedagogical solution is *not* more heroic efforts to teach discrimination. Children first must have an extended and supported experience with natural text. In my opinion there is no more important knowledge that kindergarten and first-grade teachers can gain than this, for there is no other teaching principle that is so regularly, fiercely, and disastrously violated than children's developmental concept of word.

☐ Judging Readiness to Read

This brings me now to a close of those things that children need to know in order to begin to learn to read. Notably this knowledge is of the tacit variety. It is not the sort of thing that can be programmed in a workbook or dispensed by mother from a kit alleged to perpetrate a genius. In order to learn to read, children need a reasonably intact nervous system and some general intelligence—though not a great deal of it. They need also sustenance and responsibility. Regarding written language specifically, they must know its office and feel its impact on their lives. They must have time to assimilate the grammar of written language and the featural potential of written symbols. Finally, they must build a concept of word as a bound figure, comprised in English, at least, of discrete letters marching left to right.

Teachers must be ready to judge the adequacy of each child's understanding and competency on these dimensions and be prepared to do those things necessary to allow for the unfolding of such knowledge where deficiencies exist. This may sound like a difficult undertaking, but I submit that it is not. And I offer the following example to illustrate how anyone of us could reach such judgments about the "readiness" of first grade children.

My friend and professional cohort for many years, Mrs. Melvin Lee, hereafter referred to as Betty or Mrs. Lee, is a first grade teacher of great competence. She begins each school year somewhat after this fashion. She greets each child and escorts him to a desk of his own. She applies to the desk his name printed clearly on tag board and invites him to look at a storybook that was placed there in advance. At this point she already knows a number of things about this child. Did he come to the room on *his own* or was he dragged there clinging to the apron strings? Did he look her in the eye and say, "How do you do?" or glare at the floor in confusion? Did he look at or interact with other children? Did he know his name in print or any of the letters in it? And what of the book? Did he throw it on the floor, eat it, look at it, read it?

Of course she does not make penciled notes of every first impression, nor does she or would you remember exactly every single child, but these judgments are nonetheless made. And they strike, as I think one can see, at the vital resources of maturity, self-reliance, and language knowledge.

When all the children are arrayed at random to seats, their own "home base," she teaches them how to get up, push in their chairs, pull them out, and sit down again. She takes the time that is needed to have this mastered perfectly (or at least nearly perfectly). And in this the seeds of trust are sown—order, discipline, responsibility. Next, she introduces the children to their classroom, pointing out what things are, where and how they may be used. This ends with a tour of some ten or twelve "work" centers at which individual children may carry out interesting and informative tasks—drawing, making puzzles, alphabet matching, clay modeling, and the like. The children then return to their seats (practicing lesson one), and the class is divided, again at random, into two groups. Group One is sent to the work centers, and Group Two assembles in a corner of the room where they will work with Mrs. Lee examining and talking about a box turtle and dictating a group story about it. Thereafter, the groups are swapped, and Group One examines a different turtle, perhaps a slider, while Group Two works at the centers. Betty takes whatever time is needed to make sure that the children know how to move naturally from one place of business to another. Later, the children make illustrations for the stories they dictated, and later still the whole class, comfortably sprawled on the floor, listens to the *Tale of Timothy Turtle* read aloud by Mrs. Lee. On the following day the stories and pictures are shared—read aloud chorally with Betty's help and individually by those who are able to do so.

So much for a glimpse of one first grade school beginning. I think from it you can see that by the end of the first two or three days of school Betty or you or I may know the general maturity of each child we have in our charge. Does he follow directions or not? Can he work alone at a task? For how long? With what interest? Does he examine things like turtles and the other paraphernalia of the classroom with discernment? How does he talk about such matters? Was his dictated construction a sentence or a fragment—or did he, perhaps, speak not a word? How did he respond at story time? Did he cuddle into it or watch the fly on the wall instead? Did he choral-read the dictated account; did he read some sentences alone? Did he identify individual words? Did he remember them?

It is by this means that we know when children will begin to acquire a sight vocabulary and begin to learn to read. Until they have such underlying knowledge and inner sense of where they are bound, we must do those things that will help build such knowledge. Do they not listen to storybooks that are read to them? Then you must tell them a story, for that's the more ancient way. Try "Rumplestiltskin" and you will reach them. I have seen it, and I know it to be so. Compared to these kinds of understandings and judgments, the standard tests of readiness are pale, misleading stuff. The surface of things will not serve us unless we can bring to bear our understanding of the knowledge underlying the actions of each child.

The Beginning Reader

The beginning phase of learning to read is an incredibly fascinating period. Years ago it seemed to me one of the major miracles of human learning, and, of course, in a very real sense it is. Yet today I believe that I can understand it somewhat better. The striking thing about it is its suddenness of onset. One day a child is simply not reading. He may be reciting familiar stories while turning the pages of a book or following the teacher in rereading a dictated account, but true contact with the printed text is simply not there. The next day, suddenly he is. Memory still largely assists him, but his forward progress in reading is clearly under the control of the words that he identifies. It is my belief that the store of tacit knowledge of the pre-reading child awaits, as it were, release until that time that word boundaries are discerned and the concept of word is attained. Thereafter, the dividing line between nonreading and reading is crossed at a rush.

This beginning period is a somewhat delicate one for the learner and requires, in my opinion, very sensitive management on the part of the teacher. As the bass fisherman feels that first delicate message from his line and marshals his senses to tell him when the hook may be set, so the teacher now must call on his full experience with children making this beginning and avoid rough handling and clumsy acts. A consideration of how children learn to read when they do so on their own is helpful in this regard.

☐ The Natural Beginning

Children learning to read on their own have two enormous advantages. First, there is little or no external pressure requiring that they do so or do so to any particular standard. Second, they are both free to set their own standard and accustomed to doing it without full apprehension in a communicative setting. The child at the dinner table discriminates between grown-up talk and that which is directed to him. He is quite forgiving in this. He permits the babble to go by, sampling from it what his mind and fancy chooses and discarding the rest. It was a good number of years before I knew as a child the difference between a bond market and a fish market. I supposed there was a difference, but precisely what, I really didn't particularly care.

I am convinced that children do have a quite high tolerance for this kind of ambiguity and a cheery satisfaction with that part that they then can make sense of. Such a posture should serve them well in learning to read. On their own they may shift at will from recitation to reading, from demanding that the text "work," to letting it go by the board. They may fix on a word and ponder what it is or skip it altogether and get on with the game. If an adult is nearby or an older child, they may ask for a word and usually they are told it directly. So gradually their sight vocabulary grows, and as it does, they may demand more of the text and of individual words themselves. Altogether this condition seems to me quite ideal. It should serve well as a guide to us when we direct the beginning reader formally.

In the classroom setting, of course, there are external pressures. Children know that they are expected to learn to read and that we are eager (sometimes even frantic) to have them do so. They know also which of their peers are stars and which are snails. What they do not know is that learning to read *is* a very natural thing for children in a literate culture to do and that each will achieve it in time as the conditions for doing so are met. It is absolutely imperative, I think, that we convey this confidence to children in our every act and deed.

Unfortunately, the tendency over the years has been to set very rigid standards, many of which are grossly inappropriate and, in terms of my understanding of the reading process, quite nonsensical. Demanding auditory discrimination responses for phonemic elements of words before words themselves are conceptually stable is one example among many. Moreover, today, when our well-intentioned but often ill-conceived standards of quality are firmly applied, teachers are driven blindly to realize the *appearance* of knowledge in children to the neglect of the true and underlying knowledge upon which the whole enterprise depends. This circumstance simply must be changed. The right kinds of standards must be set, in the right way and at the right time, for each child.

☐ Supported Beginning Reading

Once the "miracle of reading" has happened, I believe it important that children continue to read as abundantly as possible in a carefully supported setting. It matters little whether this be in storybooks or dictated accounts, well-known songs, poems, even prayers, so long as the children have a reasonable recall of and commitment to the content they are dealing with. Obviously, it is desirable that the text be in language that is semantically and syntatically honest. It is for this reason that I find the distorted structure of most preprimers undesirable and have tended to find pupil-dictated accounts, supplemented by good trade books, the more versatile material.

As the teacher listens to the beginner read aloud, he must be prepared to make a host of field decisions based on his judgment of what the child knows and what he is trying to do. It is exciting work, never, of course, done perfectly. It is also quite difficult to describe and impossible to prescribe. Roughly it goes like this. Given that the child is "in contact" with the print, I may help him to continue to read by tracking his voice on the page with a moving pointer. If he pauses at a word, I try to discern what he is doing—does he reread and then forge ahead; does he skip and then pick up the theme?—in either case, I would let him go on. If he is at a standstill, I might reread for him, pause, and if the word did not come to him, supply it. On the other hand, if the state of his recall is weak and his sight vocabulary meager, I might voice in each needed word after only the slightest pause, in order to keep the reading going as fully fused with meaning and syntax as possible. It is quite like holding up the beginning swimmer giving just enough support but no more than is needed for the act to be articulated.

The trick in this form of support reading lies in making, in so far as it is possible to do so, true natural reading occur. The teacher capitalizes on the pupil's recall of text, his demand for meaning, and knowledge of written language, including word knowledge, and helps him bring all of this to bear on the task. In order to do this, of course, aids must be given reasonably quickly and appropriately so that the show may be kept going. Blind recall out of contact with print and heedless rather than heedful attention to words is not wanted. Equally unwanted is a disintegrated naming of one word after another, filled with stops, stammers, and wild guesses. The teacher must steer the beginner between this Scylla and Charybdis.

While new books and new dictations are continually added, loved storybooks may be read over and over, first with the teacher's help and then alone. The same may be done with a compilation of the child's dictations. Repetition of this kind is no more boring to children than any other over-and-over again activity that they naturally indulge in. It is important to conceptualize and to direct such rereadings as in fact *rereadings*, not as conditioning exercises for memorizing words. This distinction is critical. Reading does not emerge from a sight vocabulary. Quite the other way around, vocabulary emerges from reading. This tenet holds, moreover, not only at this tender stage but throughout life.

☐ Acquiring a Sight Vocabulary

During this period, children begin to acquire a sight vocabulary, and the rate of acquisition of that vocabulary undergoes a steady change. The benchmark that I use to denote the conclusion of this support reading period is a simple one. When children acquire nearly all new words occurring in their dictated accounts and remember them reliably, they are ready to venture into reading material that is not supported by memory.

A record of this progression is easily maintained by use of the word bank as described in Chapter 1. After the child has had three or four days of supported practice with a selection, the teacher picks those words that he believes the child may *know* and presents them to him in isolation. Those he can identify go in the bank; those he cannot are discarded. The bank is composed only of words that the child does, in this sense, know.

☐ Prephonetic and Letter-Name Concepts of Word

Our studies of children's invented spellings suggest a good deal about the nature of children's concept of word at this beginning-to-read phase. Some examples taken from a recent study at our center will help make these characteristics more clear. Richard Gentry (1977a) composed a list of words so that a variety of error types could be studied in relation to grade, kindergarten through second, and to three levels of achievement within each grade. He administered these to 180 children, 60 at each grade and 20 at each level. In Chart 1 are shown some productions by three kindergarten children. Child 1 makes no response or now and then a vague scribble. Child 2 produces writing-like symbols mixed with some numbers and letters in various orientations which he composes left to right or right to left as the spirit moves him. Child 3 seems a bit more advanced. He codes the initial phoneme for each word quite accurately, but stops there. I infer that all three of these children know a good bit about written language, but I doubt very much that the concept of word has yet crystallized and stabilized for them.

Chart 1. Inventive Spellings by Three Prereading Children at Progressive Stages of Word Knowledge

KEY	CHILD		
	1	2	3
monster	ᴍᴍ	← 3 N ᴀ ᴢ	m
united			u
dressing	ʒ ᴜ	← ++ʀoᴇ	JR
bottom	ᴄᴡ		b
hiked		→ HN̄ᴛ+ᴇ	h
human	ʒ	ᴢᴄ	h
eagle			
closed			
number			n
peeked			
sink			
bumpy			

The productions of three more kindergarteners are shown in Chart 2. The difference between this set and the first is clear cut. For children 1 and 3, each word has a beginning and an end. The phonemes are, for the most part, correctly entered left to right by representative letter names. (Child 1's labeling human as *bm* stems from the fact that this word was given in the sentence, "The *bionic man* is human," all of which indicates clearly the instability of the word concept at this stage.) There are, moreover, deviant responses and omissions, both for phonemes having and not having an alaphabet letter name. I infer that for these children the concept of word has begun to stabilize and that they are beginning to develop a letter-name strategy, even though this performance is still somewhat shaky.

Now examine the work of the three first graders shown in Chart 3. Here we see an almost perfect example of what J. Beers has called the letter-name strategy. Words are spelled with remarkable consistency, with named letters matched to the phonetic elements of the word. Where the phoneme has no letter name, a consistent substitution is made, as in *e* for short *i*, children 2 and 3, for example. Moreover, there is full evidence of the acceptance of the economy and abstractness of spelling as described by Read (1975) in the children's omissions of preconsonantal nasals—and their treatment of the vocalic consonants *l* and *r*. It is interesting to note that the earlier match of *j* for *dr* as employed by children in Chart 2 has now changed for these children to the conventional *dr* of English.

The transition between the examples in Chart 2 and Chart 3 is one that occurs during the beginning-to-read phase. Once the concept of word is stabilized, children begin to acquire words on a sight basis,

Chart 2. Inventive Spellings of Three Children for Whom the
Concept of Word Has Begun to Crystallize

KEY	CHILD		
	1	2	3
monster	msd	m	mst
united	na		unte
dressing	jsn	s	jrsn
bottom	bl	b	bdm
hiked	hi	I.	ht
human	bm (bionic man)	m	umn
eagle	iat (deviant)	e	egl
closed	iat (deviant)	c	KLZ
number	ia (deviant)	m	NBR
peeked	p	p	PER
sink	s	s	SE
bumpy	bt	b	BP

Chart 3. Inventive Spellings by Three Children Who Have
Mastered the Concept of Word and Spell Phonetically by Letter Name

KEY	CHILD			
	1	2	3	4
monster	MOTH	MOSTR	MOSTR	MONSTR
united	UNITED	UNINT	UNITT	UNITID
dressing	DRESSING	GASIN	JESIN	GESG
bottom	BODM	BODUM	BDIM	BOOM
hiked	HITE	HIT	HIET	HIKT
human	HUMN	CUMU	HUEN	HYWMEN
eagle	IGL	EGO	EGL	EGL
closed	CLOSED	COST	KLUS	CLOSD
number	NUBR	NOMR	NUMBER	NOMBR
peeked	PIC	PET	PIT	PEKT
sink	SINK	SEC	SEK	SIK
bumpy	BUBI	BOMBE	BUPBEE	BUPY

and these they typically spell correctly. At the same time they tacitly
build this marvelously consistent and abstract theory of English spelling. Chart 4 is an example of some "creative" writing by a kindergar-
tener and a first grader during this beginning period. Some words were
correctly spelled; the remaining misspelled words are almost wholly
predictable given the letter-name theory. Such is the miracle of beginning to read and write.

Chart 4. Compositions by Two Beginning Readers Who Employ a
Letter-Name Strategy to Spell Words They Do Not Yet Know by Sight

---

DONALD

DONALD HATS ME. DONALD LIKES JOHN.
DONALD LIKES PLAG SOKR DONALD ALLWAS
bregs A SNAK.

My TEETH

Las nit I pold out my lustuth and
I pot in ondr my pelr. And wan I wok
up I fid a two dilr bel. THE END

☐ Beginning Writing

There is in this developmental sequence a great naturalness, and so in
directing children's writing the teacher must exercise the same kind of
judgment and tact that is required in supporting their beginning efforts
to read. Clearly, children need much opportunity to scribble, draw,
and experiment freely with graphics. A device used by Mrs. Lee in her
first grade has always struck me as particularly well chosen.

On the corner of a table she keeps a supply of blank newsprint
paper cut to a convenient size, about eight inches by eight inches.
She calls this "waiting paper" and teaches the children that whenever
they have "nothing to do" they may come, take a piece of waiting
paper, and put on it anything they please. The only rule is that they
must fill both sides and keep what they have done in their work folder.
It is truly fascinating to examine a child's waiting-paper work over a
school year. Some, as you would guess, begin with crude scribbles
and end with notes quite confidential and sincere.

During the beginning-to-read period, children will already have
learned the alphabet, and most will begin to attempt writing on their
own. It is my feeling that a dictated experience story setting is ideal
for nurturing this transition. If the teacher's plan includes well-chosen
and carefully examined experiences or activities, these provide excellent content for beginning writing efforts. Some children ask for paper
so they can write for themselves; others require much encouragement
and support. Not surprisingly, their reluctance usually stems from their
sad misconception that they do not know how to spell. That tragic
albatross of behaviorism, that misspelling begets misspelling, still
hangs about many a parent's and many a teacher's neck.

To allay children's fears on this matter, I find it helpful to have them
compose a story or two as a group, letting them decide jointly how
each word should be spelled. In this way they learn that if someone
happens to "know" the correct form, one should use it, of course, but

if not, the thing to do is to invent the best rendering they can. Once children have made this beginning, I believe it best *not* to supply "possibly needed words" in advance. Furthermore, after they have written, I do not correct their spellings. To do either, it seems to me, merely reinforces the false implication that they should know at this beginning stage how to spell every word they can speak.

Critiques of the children's writing are given both individually and in a small-group session. Often they read each other's work, for interestingly, children who are spelling in similar ways can read these compositions more readily than an adult who is unfamiliar with the form. Emphasis is placed largely on the intrinsic interest and fullness of the effort, or on the fresh insight and observations that different writers have achieved. Concern for correctness is limited to letter formation and spacing (with due regard for individual differences in these matters) and occasionally to spelling when, in my judgment, the pupil "knows" the word and has misspelled it or when I judge that a better inventive effort might have been made.

☐ Word Study Rationale

As children are advancing through the beginning-to-read period and becoming fairly consistent letter-name spellers, I introduce a formal word-study program. That I should do so is as shocking to some as it would be to many others if I did not. Accordingly, let me explain my position on this matter as clearly as I can. What I advocate here may look superficially like a traditional program of phonics, but it is not. Moreover, I am convinced that it is this surface similarity that has yielded to phonics instruction the good effects it has achieved, albeit for reasons quite different from those believed in by its advocates.

Many children do learn both to read and to spell acceptably in perfectly natural and almost altogether tacit ways. Others, however, do not, nor do I think their failure can be attributed to abnormality of mind, except in rare cases. Bad, or rather, ill-timed instruction doubtless takes it toll, but I also believe that a fair number of children simply do not examine words with much care. In order to read, they really do not need to do so. Moreover, as fluency in reading is gained, the sampling of graphic features is quite naturally ever more minimal (Smith 1971). As a consequence, reading, in and of itself, will not guarantee that the underlying order of orthography is noted and internally organized by a pupil.

From both personal and clinical experience, I know that correct spelling is not learned by sheer memory nor is it learned mechanically from rules. Our research suggests instead that some underlying abstract orderings are gradually acquired as a function of developing intellectual maturity and a prolonged experience with written language. I assume that these orderings are ultimately of the kind postulated by Chomsky and Halle (1968) in their theory of phonological competence. Knowledge of this kind can be conceived of only as tacit knowledge; it cannot be taught directly or expressed concretely at any of its stages.

Nonetheless, what is learned cannot be learned in any other way than through the examination of words. Since this is not done automatically by many children, for a host of different reasons, and since the acts simply of reading and writing do not guarantee that they *will* be done, I believe that formal activities should be staged so that words will, in fact, be examined.

The word-study activities that I propose are altogether different from the so-called decoding skills. I do not think, in fact, that there are any such things as decoding skills, for decoding is a process that is done by the skillful in a way far too complicated for any of us to describe. In these word-study activities there is no skill to be learned but instead simply an activity, usually an arraying task, to be performed. These tasks are arranged in a rough sequence as one finds empirically that children at different stages of reading/language development can do them. It is assumed that the performance of these tasks is sufficient to induce the wanted apprehension, while the names or labels given to the tasks are recognized as surface stuff, relatively arbitrary and in themselves nonessential to the underlying substrate of knowledge being formed.

☐ Word Study for Beginning Readers

During the beginning-to-read period, specifically when children are acquiring an initial sight vocabulary and doing so at a progressive rate, I introduce the study of initial consonants and consonant clusters. There is no thought on my part that I am "teaching children their beginning sounds." They know these already, as is clearly evident in their invented spellings. What I am teaching them indirectly are three things. First, this activity implies that words are objects that may be examined in various ways. Second, it suggests that in addition to being bound figures with letters and phonemic elements marching through them, one-syllable words may be categorized as having two logical parts, the consonant elements, if any, that precede the vowel and the vowel and what follows. Finally, this activity conveys a distinctive feature of vowels since they alone recur at this critical point of division.

This objective may be achieved in many different ways. My present choice is roughly as follows. We use a typical consonant sound chart and also a smaller desk-size replica. On the big chart we teach children how to run through their word bank, finding words that begin like the various pictures and letter-keyed words. The child may have the word *band* in his bank. He finds the picture of the *ball* on the chart and says, "Band and ball begin with the letter *b*," perhaps holding the beginning letter of *band* directly under the key letter *b* that accompanies the pictured *ball*. When the children learn the procedure they may do it on their own at their seats, helping each other if they wish.

The next series of exercises is quite standard in reading instruction, but ours is considerably more open ended than can be managed in a workbook format. Mrs. Lee has designed the sequence in a four-step set of activities. She chooses four initial consonants, perhaps *b, m, r,* and *s*, and prints them on a 5" x 8" card. Beneath this she draws the symbol ⊂⊃ which means "get the box of pictures labeled BMRS and sort them under the letter headings." When the task is completed, she checks the pupils' work. The children then mix the pictures up and return them in the box to its place on the shelf.

On a second 5" x 8" card the same letters are again printed and beneath them the symbols shown at right, which mean (1) get a piece of paper and put your name on it and (2) get a pencil and draw as many pictures of things that begin with these letters as you can think of. The children label each picture with its initial letter and draw a line to denote the remainder of the word. As Betty checks their work, the children read the pictures to her, and she completes the label. Thus, *monkey* becomes as shown in the margin. These papers are preserved in the child's work folder.

The third task is handled in much the same manner, but this time the symbol shown in margin designates that the children are to get a magazine, find pictures of things that begin with the target letters, cut them out, paste them on their paper, and again label them. Finally, the fourth card directs the children to review their word bank and separate out all words they know that begin with the letters *B, M, R,* and *S*. They then read these to Betty, and the activity sequence is complete.

Betty teaches these procedures to her pupils with great care. She demonstrates to a small group in the reading circle how it is to be done, sometimes beginning with just a single letter or a pair of letters, and the children may then practice as a group at their seats. It is most important that she demonstrate the prodecures. It is not the discrimination that is here being learned, but the conscious act of focusing on the word object in a different way. For most children the experience is a new and challenging experience. When Betty is confident that the children know how to proceed, she then assigns them to the four letter cards, and they work through the sequence on their own.

The cards are arrayed on a wall at a suitable height and near a work table. The full sequence includes initial single consonants, digraphs, and blends. As the children work at these tasks, Betty is interested not only in the accuracy of their judgments but their fluency and flexibility in responding. As productivity and speed increase, she may allow some to skip steps one and two and thus move through the tasks more quickly. Typically, children complete this sequence at that time when supported reading is no longer needed and they are making the transition into a basal reader or some similar collection.

Monkey

Sustaining Instruction

At the close of this stage, pupils are able to begin to read books. The wonderfully complex things that precede this task have already taken place. The miracle itself has occurred. And now that beginning period when they depend upon memory and their teacher for support is accomplished.

Curiously, these events that I have tried to describe in detail and at some length may happen very rapidly. Some children come to school already reading; they have done these preliminary things pretty much on their own. Others come to school as nonreaders but frolic through the stages in just a few months. Inevitably, however, there will be a good number of children who require many months or even several years of careful instruction before they begin to read. No one, I think, would deny that it is the community's wish, the principal's obligation, and the teacher's clear professional duty to see to it that such instruction is forthcoming. But herein lies a great source of conflict—a whole Pandora's box of anxiety, anger, and grief; denials, demands, and disillusionment.

It is inevitable that conflict should be the outcome when the reading program is planned and evaluated on the basis of a rigid timetable of packaged skills. It is also inevitable that there will be conflict and misunderstanding if teachers and parents do not know what children *must* know in order to read. My hope is that the "benchmark" events described in this chapter will serve as a guide.

Children's invented spellings provide a clear and reliable index of the quality and power of their word knowledge upon which reading progress depends. Drawing, scribble-writing, and semirandom lettering precede beginning reading. Knowledge of word as a bound figure is demonstrated when a child can point to and name words in a dictation or an easy story that he has been helped to "read." The letter-name spellings accompany the early beginning-to-read period. At this time, children will acquire, without stress or undue memorization efforts, a beginning sight vocabulary. It is as easy as that. The parents, the principal, and the teacher can observe the child's work and *know* where he stands in this progression. Thereafter it is up to the teacher to support and contrive instruction that is rigorous, intriguing, and sustained. Such is the art of teaching; with knowledge and understanding it will prosper, with ignorance and distrust it will fail and so will children.

Teaching Children Who Can Read

6

Between what we term beginning reading and early reading an interesting period of transition must take place. During the former period, full teacher support must be given in order that the beginner can assess text. As a concept of word is formed and a beginning sight vocabulary accrues, the need for formal support gradually decreases. A knowledge of word characterized by spelling inventions of the letter-name type makes it certain that new words can be attended to and remembered. Yet this knowledge base is still primitive so that words will not be acquired and retained as easily as they will be later on. Once children have learned to read simple material without assistance and have begun to master the pattern concept for short vowels a change in word power occurs.

Early Reading Instruction

Reading that is supported by memory (as in dictated accounts or stories that have been listened to) is no longer needed when children have a sight vocabulary of several hundred words and when their ability to acquire "new" words in the supported setting is smooth and stable. What they now must learn is to trust their anticipation of what will be written as they test this against what in fact is before them in text. It is for this reason that I think it so important that primary reading materials be written in natural language, easily apprehensible to children at this general level of maturity. It is for this reason also that I think these materials should be informative and appealing to the mind. If they are stories, they should get somewhere. If they are jokes or riddles or jingles, they should amuse, surprise, or delight the listener. Where syntax, meaning, and form are distorted, the result is that anticipation fades and the process of reading must disintegrate into an isolated naming of words.

☐ Early Reading Materials

As noted in Chapter 2, the liberalizing of the vocabulary controls in contemporary readers has resulted in better-written material at this level. But I do not think we have gone far enough in this reform. So long as writing is hobbled by formula and produced by inexperienced rather than experienced children's authors, we will teach less effectively than we could. Consider, if you will, this horrendous blunder in a fourth grade reader that is now mercifully out of print. In one story a cat is fed milk and then said to have rubbed against the legs of the feeder as if to say "thank you." No cat this side of creation ever did such a thing in its life. Cats rub *before* they are fed. Afterwards they are as undemonstrative as stone. They are contemptuous, ungrateful creatures; it is their nature and their charm to be so. I find distortions of this kind profoundly disturbing.

I believe that publishers would welcome the opportunity to prepare better works for early readers. It is our responsibility to persuade them that better works are needed. In the meantime, I pick the best selectively and supplement them with a large number of storybooks. I do this because I feel that I do need a set of relatively short selections that may be read by a group of beginning readers.

☐ Initiating the Reading Lesson

Because children at this stage have been read aloud to extensively and have read, with support, many storybooks themselves, they now know what books are and how they work. Therefore, I am able to follow from the beginning the general teaching plan described earlier, which Stauffer has termed the directed reading-thinking activity.

When children are gathered at the reading circle, I give each one a book and explain the ground rules. I tell them that they will use these books to practice reading in order to learn to do so better. I explain further that these books contain many stories and articles that they will probably find interesting but that these selections are to be used only in reading circle and as they are assigned. Should they wish to read for pleasure or research, they are to use the classroom library. Finally, I tell them that in these lessons I will always be most interested in what they think each selection will be about, what they learn from their reading, and what they can say to each other about what they have learned. This may sound like heavy talk for six year olds, but I really do believe that when our teaching purpose is serious, we should declare it to children directly and then honor that statement in the procedures that follow.

My next step is to have the children turn at once to the story I have selected. Then I set about the task of eliciting their ideas as to what it will be about. I advise them to read the title and to think about what it may signify and look at the pictures and construct for themselves the scene these imply. This is accomplished with the simplest of questions—"What do you think a story with a title like this might be about?" "Look at these two pictures. What seems to be happening here? What do you think might happen next?" It is truly amazing how productive and varied childrens' ideas can be even in the very first session of this kind. Also, it is fascinating to see the things that they do not do. Many, for example, will construct altogether different themes for the title and the pictures, with no seeming awareness that the two must mesh. Similarly with plot and counterplot, they will discard the first theme on discerning the second and be genuinely surprised when the two come together at the end. And, of course, it is this, the structure and form of the genre, that they must learn through examined experiences in reading many different kinds of selections over the years.

When the children have constructed the best set of anticipations they can, I tell them to read, each for himself, a certain number of pages. My decision as to how far they are to read is based each time on the fullness and reach of their predictions. In the beginning it may be but a page or two. At this stage most of the children read in an audible whisper. This will gradually diminish to silent reading as they gain confidence and power over the months. I observe them carefully and give support as it is needed. Once again, the teacher at this point must be adroit and judicious, giving just the right amount of help at the right speed. The guiding principle, however, is to be helpful and make reading possible for each child.

When all have finished, I may ask them to rectify what they thought originally with what they have learned from reading. "Did things go as you thought they would? How were they different?" On the other hand, if no rectification is needed, I may say, "You were right in what you thought, weren't you? Now what do you think will happen next?" And so again I elicit their best anticipations. In this way we proceed to the conclusion.

In most present-day readers, stories are about six pages in length and can be completed in a twenty-minute lesson. I am never concerned about finishing a story in one session, however, for I find it perfectly simple to stop and pick up the theme again on the following day. In any event, when the story has been read and predictions are confirmed, I try first to tease out some judgment for the children to wrestle with. "Did the little girl actually win the race? Did the foxes really talk? What do you think of the way Mother handled her problem with Tommy?" Questions of this kind lead to commitment, reason, and often rereading for evidential support. I am never interested in recitation and reject it when children offer it—"You are telling me what happened. I want to know what you think about what happened." Beautiful insights often emerge from discussions of this kind.

I recall well the time that one child differed with her classmates' assertion that Mother had been right to make Tommy clean up the kitchen after his dog had tracked up the floor. "It seems a shame," she said. "He'd wanted that dog so much and now he doesn't want him anymore. And besides he couldn't clean the kitchen right anyway." Thus, did justice of the eye for eye and tooth for tooth variety come under the scrutiny of a first-grade mind. "How then do you think Mother might have gotten a better result?" I asked. Far be it for me to enter the fray and lay down some judgment on the permissiveness issue. I am content that children read and think.

I have written at length about Stauffer's directed reading-thinking activity in the setting of early reading instruction in order to emphasize that this plan is used from the beginning. When the shift is made from the memory support of beginning reading to support by anticipation and purpose, the teacher must have a means of manipulating and monitoring that anticipation. By staging instruction in this manner, children's tacit knowledge of the world, including their knowledge of written language as it conveys ideas and events of that world, is rendered overt and observable both for the children and the teacher. As these anticipations are seen to grow in maturity, reach, flexibility, and appropriateness, the material of instruction may be varied in complexity and genre. This is the underlying source of reading power, and like all tacit knowledge, we cannot touch it directly, yet we may know it and exercise it in coherent acts of this kind.

It should be emphasized that these reading lessons are not the only reading that takes place in this plan. Indeed they are but a small part of it. Children are assigned time to read in books of their own selection and helped to do so. Formal teaching time in the reading circle is devoted to discussion about who is reading what and why and what difference it has made. There is reading also, both free and assigned, in relation to topical curricular areas: science, social studies, and the like. Moreover, purposeful writing continues, as do formal activities of word study.

☐ Vocabulary, Decoding, and Aids to Word Recognition

In describing the directed reading-thinking activity I omitted any mention of vocabulary, for this reason: Word knowledge is the result, not the cause of reading. If children cannot deal conceptually with the ideas and issues before them, then you must simply find another book. If they can, given the prerequisite sight vocabulary and level of word knowledge described earlier, then their anticipatory discussions will ready them for the specific context at hand. Moreover, it is precisely the utility of anticipation for the perception of written language that I want them to experience. Accordingly, I do not pre-teach either concepts or words. There is no need, of course, to be doctrinaire about this; exceptions can be made. If the name of the principal character is unusual, perhaps a foreign spelling, I might well read it to them and explain how it works. On the other hand I might not, just to see what they do on their own.

In my opinion, far too much emphasis has been placed on sounding words out. Surface analysis makes it abundantly clear that a word may not be sounded out on a linear, phoneme-by-phoneme basis. It is the complex inner orderings of words, themselves composed of semantic, syntactic, and phonemic properties, that underlies our ability to name them. Moreover, we simply do not know in any measured way the means we employ to do so. As the mature reader reads with the will to comprehend, this orthographic knowledge functions in concert with all else that he knows of language and the world to achieve immediate meaning. When these competencies are incomplete, occasions will arise when a word is met that will not yield to the force of anticipation and for which the present state of orthographic knowledge is inadequate. This is the state of affairs when the early reader points to a word and says, "I'm stuck, what's that?"

At that point, what should a teacher do? My judgment about this battle-scarred question is this: It seems to me, first, that we should ascertain whether or not the "will to comprehend" and the "anticipatory disposition" is in order. This is a complicated way of saying a familiar maxim of reading instruction—"Is the pupil making use of context clues?" The teacher can easily note whether or not the context or syntax is likely to cue the correct or a synonymous identification. If this is so, the reader either missed the message earlier and/or had ceased to demand understanding. In this case, I might suggest that the pupil reread, or I might reread the section for him, pausing as described earlier, and letting him fill the gap. Alternatively, it might seem to me that this rehearsal will require more time than is warranted. In that case I might elect to tell the pupil the word immediately and urge him forward. The troublesome word should then be explored in group session after the story has been completed.

If it appears that context of the story will not help, then it may be reasonably assumed either that the pupil's confidence and interest has faltered or that he does not know enough, orthographically, to identify the word. In this circumstance, the teacher is on very uncertain ground, for he cannot know in any precise way what aspect of word knowledge may serve. My decision here is to *guess*, but it is, I hope, an educated guess.

As I have tried to show in this and the preceding chapter, our research and that of many others has provided us with a global view and feel for children's knowledge of words as this progresses developmentally. If a child is inventing spellings that fall pretty clearly into the "letter-name" category, it would seem to me very doubtful indeed that the vowel element of the word *pit* would be available to him. Were he to invent the word *pit*, he would spell it *pet*. Were he to "sound this word out" he would get "*Pu. I. Tu,*" which is nothing, and were he to "blend" this business together, by some chance he might come up with *pite*, which will not do either. In this circumstance it seems to me that the sensible thing to do would be to say, "That word is *pit*," and get on with the reading.

Suppose, however, that this same child is moving out of the letter-name phase. He tends now to invent more and more short vowels correctly and shows evidence of some awareness of vowel markers. In this case he *will* have, on a sight basis, a fair number of short *i* words. Then why not remind him of this condition? I might then write the word *sit* on a card and place it beneath the unidentified word *pit*. As with every aid, if it works, fine; if not, I would forget it and tell him the word.

With children at this general level I do not hesitate to show them syllable divisions and see if this will help them identify a word. I might occlude the inflectional ending and see if the base word is known. And even though it may sound inconsistent, I do sometimes reread the sentence and form the initial consonant of the word to be identified. In short, I will do most anything I please if I think it may help in that circumstance.

There are, on the other hand, a good number of commonly employed aids that I think are silly, and I avoid them. I never say to a child, "Look for the little word that you know in the big word." Try that on *Tomato* and see where it leads you! I am well aware that spelling the word out, naming the letters, is often effective. It seems to settle the child down and hold him to the task, with the result that the word sometimes comes to him. I avoid this however, because it strikes me as regressive, that is, it is a thing that he *can* do for himself anyway. (It is the underlying strategy of his knowledge of word). What he needs is to move forward from this point, not backwards. I try never to say "sound it out," for I believe this makes dangerous and false implications about how words are identified. Instead I say, "Does this help?" or "Try it this way." Finally I try to weed from my repertoire of aids those that depend on the child's prior knowledge of the word to be identified. These false aids are remarkably common and altogether useless.

The child says, "I don't know that word," pointing to the word *know*. The teacher replies, "Oh, yes you do; you just said it." True, perhaps, but hardly grist for advancing word knowledge. For another example, the child might ask for the word *blew* in the sentence, "The wind blew and blew." To say "What do you think the wind did?" would be fine, but to make the sound "puff, puff" would not. An even worse approach for arriving at the word "blew" would be to ask, "What color is your dress?" Yet indeed I have heard this done.

These then are the aids I would and would not give as I observed early readers in a directed reading-thinking activity. I do one further thing toward vocabulary development after the story is completed. First I ask the children if they had difficulty with any words or if they learned any words they did not know before. Then I encourage them to tell, in so far as they are able, how they worked them out. Children learn much from such discussions and so do teachers. Next I might replay such aids as I may have given, showing what was done or what might have been done. Finally I might relate these aids to the word-study activities that the children are engaged in, if this seems appropriate.

☐ Word Study for Early Readers

The word-study program described for beginning readers continues on a formal basis during this early reading period. When the children have completed the discrimination sequences for the initial consonants and blends, I teach them the term *vowel* and show what letters it designates. It is amusing to see how quickly this is learned, for they already know tacitly what vowels are, this being a necessary criterion for the initial consonant concept. Now they need merely to attach a label to the thing known.

Working first with children in the reading circle and later at their seats, I may have them sort their word bank holdings first by number of syllables. This, incidentally, is a discrimination that early readers can learn to do quite readily, provided the teacher is reasonably flexible and allows them to respond to their own language. For little Richmond, Virginia, children *poor* pronounced *po or* often falls in the two syllable slot, as does *cat* when it is pronounced *KA et*. I usually say, "Yes, the way you say it I hear two parts too. The way I say it, it sounds more to me like one," and let it go at that.

Next I may ask the children to sort the single syllable words that are printed on their word bank cards into two groups—those that have a single vowel and those with more than one vowel. Then I will ask them to select from the single vowel group all those with *a* and put them in a pack. In due course these are brought to the reading circle. I introduce the common short vowel pattern for *a* as in *bat* and have the children find words in their packets with the same pattern match of the vowel and closing consonant or consonant cluster. They listen each time for their own pronunciation of the vowel element.

The trick in managing this kind of exercise is to treat it like a concept development task and to be flexible in handling the children's decisions. I might, for example, have accepted exemplars such as *pat* and *tack* and written them on the chalkboard. Then a child may offer the word *pan* from his list. I might say, "Does the *a* in *pan* sound exactly like the *a* in *pat* when you say the words?" For some the answer will be yes, for others no, and both may be correct. Then I might say, "I hear a slight difference in length in *pan*, but we'll put it in our short *a* group." Next I might be offered the word *all*. I write it on the board. Then we discuss the pattern and what each hears, and I place it outside the short *a* group.

The teacher must accept the idea that the categories of speech sounds and the relationship they bear to letters and letter patterns are fuzzy, not sharply right/wrong things. They must be sorted out gradually by the children as they test their hypotheses against the grouping standard. It is not necessary that they work analytically from rule to decision. Indeed initially it may not be possible for them to do so, for note that this vowel pattern task is, on its face, a relational judgment of the kind characteristic of concrete operational thought. It will be recalled, moreover, that Zutell (1975) has shown a significant correlation between the transitional management of vowels and achievement on conventional decentration tasks.

It is not necessary to delay the study of vowel patterns until each child can be tested and shown to be mature in decentration. Such would be a gross violation of Piagetian theory. The children's word knowledge at this time is quite sufficient to make this beginning in the study of vowel patterns. They need, however, not the rule and the reason but the fact of the category before them in terms of words they now know on a slightly more primitive basis. Relational thinking, as applied to words, does not create new knowledge but itself derives from these categorizing experiences.

There can be no more felicitious setting for this kind of learning than one in which children interact in the decision process. The teacher is arbiter and final judge, but he must be constantly alert to the honest error and "reward" it as fully as the categorical match. When a child adduces a nonexemplar, I ask not in an accusative way, but with genuine curiosity, "How did you come to pick that one?" and so I learn what feature of word has attracted him.

When the children have made a beginning toward this way of grouping these words, Mrs. Lee sets them forward on another four-step short vowel discrimination series. This is very similar to the one they did with the beginning consonants earlier. First, they sort pictures of exemplars and nonexemplars. Then they draw and label, this time with the beginning element, if there is one, and the vowel. Next they cut and paste and label in the same way and finally they assemble all of their word bank words in which they believe the short *a* can be seen and heard. Thereafter, two vowels are sorted in the same way, perhaps short *a* and short *i* until the full set is completed.

☐ From Letter-Name to Transitional Concepts of Word

During this period a change will be observed in the children's invented spellings. They begin to move from a strict letter-name strategy to that which we have termed transitional. In Chart 1, taken from Richard Gentry's study (1978), one may contrast the characteristic errors of these two phases.

It is interesting, I think, to report also that Mrs. Lee has for many years noted and called to my attention a distinct change (an increase in power) in her children's reading as they begin to show a grasp of and fluency with the short vowel categorization and discrimination tasks. It does seem to me now that this is quite as it should be. To the degree that a tacit letter-name strategy influences children's expectations about new words, and I cannot help but believe that it does, the "confusability" index must run considerably higher than it will after this beginning aspect of vowel shift has been accomplished. Thus *feel* and *fill* are no longer commonly FEL but at the very least FELE and FIL which are clearly distinct word objects. Such an underlying change

Chart 1. Inventive Spellings by Three Children Showing the Progression from "Letter-Name" to Transitional Spelling Patterns

| | CHILD | | |
KEY	1	2	3
monster	MOSTR	MONSTRE	MONSTER
united	YOÚNITIT	UNINTIDE	UNITED
dressing	DESIG	JRAISING	DREESING
bottom	BÓDIM	BODOME	BOUTTOM
hiked	HOCT	HIKCTE	HIKED
human	HÍMIN	HUMUNE	HUMUN
eagle	EGL	EGLLE	EAGL
closed	CUTD	KLOSDE	CLOSED
number	NUMBR	NOMBER	NUMBER
peeked	PITE	PEPTE	PECKED
sink	SICK	SINKCE	SEAINK
bumpy	BUPEE	BOMPE	BUMMPEA

must certainly facilitate the power of acquisition and retention of words for these early readers.

These observations should in no way be interpreted as suggesting that the plan of teaching that I follow, or more specifically the word-study activities I have described, have caused these events to occur. Such a claim would be nonsense, for our studies have shown and continue to show that these progressions occur, for the most part, regardless of method. What I think fairly may be said is that these activities and this general plan constitute things that children can do at these various levels of advancement, and I believe that in doing them, the children engage in an exercise of mind that will make subsequent advancement likely. By the same token, I think it a reasonably sound guess that children who are pressed forward in early reading in a halting, meaningless fashion, and who are drilled on rules of word structure, the underpinnings of which are unavailable to them, are headed for difficulty.

The central pedagogical argument that I wish to convey is simply this. The advancement toward language competence, which in our culture includes learning to read and write, is a progressive event dependent upon each learner's immersion in and differentiation of his experience with written language. Instruction, however it is conducted, must activate, facilitate, and, above all, defer to these unfolding events. Because we cannot specify at a skills level the discrete elements that comprise this incredibly complex achievement, we must be content to observe its changing characteristics globally and suit our prescription for teaching to those things that the learner can do. It is my feeling that our work in children's advancing knowledge of word has provided a far clearer picture of this advancement in competence than we held before. It provides us, I think, with a reasonable basis for judging what a child may and may not be expected to do. Moreover, while it cannot tell us specifically what he or we should do next, it does pretty clearly suggest what things we ought *not* to do. What I have described so far is simply one way to meet these criteria.

☐ The Open Sort

There is one further word-study activity that may be started during this early reading period. We have termed it the "open sort," and it is a design that grows in usefulness over the years. In this activity we teach children how to sort known words by varied categories—meaning, syntax, orthographic pattern—encouraging them to think of different ways themselves and challenging them to figure out the category that we or a classmate may have devised. Initially this kind of gaming with words requires a good deal of teacher leadership, but it is most important, I think, that it be done. One of the perils of most phonics programs, and our own approach to word study is not immune to this, is the implication sometimes conveyed that there is but one way of looking at words, that letters and sounds are the whole story, or that structural patterns are the whole story, or that these categories we decree are rigid and without exception. These open-sort tasks make it apparent from the beginning that words are marvelously multidimensional objects whose likenesses and differences shade toward and away from each other like the colors of the spectrum and the patterns of all we perceive. Some more detailed descriptions of the open-sort technique will be given in the succeeding section.

Toward Maturity in Reading

☐ Scope of the Progression

Many will think it strange that I make the division between early reading and the march toward maturity for children this young. This level of achievement is reached by some children at the end of the first grade year, by many at the end of grade two, and nearly all by grade four. I have chosen this point of demarcation for several reasons. First of all, once this transitional stage of word knowledge is fairly reached, children can read most that is written for them with reasonable understanding. It seems to me quite like the three or four year old who is now talking. He can deliver his message quite well to his purpose and receive those that are sent to him. Of course, there is much that these early readers do not know and cannot read, but this will continue to be true until maturity is reached. The basic process is established and before them spreads the avenue of exercise, learning, and growth.

A second reason for making the division here is to emphasize the length of this learning period. Children simply are not "taught" to read by grade three, after which time they must be expected to read perfectly and spell correctly every assignment put before them. The process unfolds continuously across this full period, and it needs the facilitation of good teaching all the way.

Finally, I do not think that one should make a distinction between primary and secondary reading instruction. The process is really the same for all once children can read. Of course, there is the well-known transition cognitively between concrete operational thought and formal operations during the early teens. But this merely broadens the range of inquiry. Nowadays, it has also become fashionable to speak of primary reading and content reading, but this too is unnecessary. Doubtless the distinction arose from the low quality of the material all-to-often found in primary readers. That condition, of course, needs to be changed.

If teachers are to do an honest job, they must know all that they can about the reading and writing process from beginning to end. This holds for all teachers of whatever discipline from pre-school to high school. This is true because reading continues to be learned across all of these years, and the progress that is made will depend in important measure on the quality of the learners' experiences in all school tasks involving written language. When I began teaching, reading instruction was a kind of trade secret of primary teachers. We secondary teachers didn't know the secret, and we were not encouraged to learn it. I think today, however, we have achieved a more rational view, and I do hope that all teachers, and parents as well, will tackle this subject anew.

☐ Materials and Teaching Purposes

In the preceding section I sketched in with some detail the format of the directed reading-thinking activity. I think of this strategy as very much like a scrimmage in football. It is not the real game, though it is played pretty much as if it were. The coach, of course, may feed in plays at will, alter the circumstances to pose problems in different ways, and, of course, blow the whistle when things go wrong or even if they go right and he wants to say so. It is much the same with this reading activity, and from this comparison some fairly important implications arise. For one, because it is not the real thing and because the teacher must be chopping into it for different purposes, I prefer not to use classical selections. I want good material, honestly written, but not the very finest. These, in conscience, I choose to handle differently. Second, I must have some purpose in mind when I direct the reading in a particular way or assign the group to a particular kind of selection. It follows from this that these lessons will be quite varied and that the interruptions, aids, and follow-up chalk talks will be relevant to the purposes at hand. Finally, since it is like the real thing, pupils must be able in fact to read what I put before them and negotiate with my help such hurdles as I think to exercise them on. The material must be easy enough to read and difficult enough to challenge. To my mind, these conditions apply at every level of instruction.

Readability formulas are widely used to suit the material to the child, but, however interesting they may be in the abstract, I find them ungainly tools leading to more mystery, misery, and mismatch than good. The more practical way to find out what children can read is to find out what they do read. Also, one may easily hand a child a book, paragraph, or whatever, ask him to read it either aloud or silently, it doesn't matter, and then ask him to tell you what he understands from what he has read. Provided you have not become hardened and deafened to the sound of misplaced children struggling and stammering over their books, your subjective judgment will be far more accurate than any that can be made by formula.

The key to deciding what the teacher's purpose should be in a directed reading lesson lies in two things: (1) an understanding of the form and structure, the genre of the particular selection presented, as well as some sense of the pupils' experience with this kind of material, and (2) an understanding of individual pupils' reading-thinking style. On page 100, I observed that early readers often show by their predictions that they have no ready expectations about the connectedness and role of the title versus the opening scene as conveyed by pictures, or between plot and counterplot even in a very simple story. Heretofore, the impact of stories read to them has reached them ready-made through the inflections, gesture, and body language of the person reading to them. But to read silently, one must generate these organizing sets on one's own. This is accomplished gradually through examined experience with stories.

The directed reading-thinking activity is one in which the teacher purposely heightens such examinations. His options are roughly of two kinds. Suspecting that a particular convention may be new to pupils, he may coach them through it carefully. Suppose, for example, that the story contains a flashback. The teacher might have children read to that point and then predict what will happen. He would then have them read until the new condition is declared and stop again. There he would hold them until they worked through to an understanding of this novel state of affairs and then complete the story.

The second general approach is rather like a test. The teacher notes a condition of challenge, perhaps this time it is a rather lengthy and convoluted setting of the story scene. He wants to know how his pupils will fare with it. He puts them to the task on their own, saying perhaps, "Read straight through the story to page —. Then I will want to know what you are thinking." Predictions at this point will allow him to know who made it and who did not. When the selection is completed, a replay of what different pupils thought, and why, will inform the less experienced about how others dealt with the problem.

Once again, it seems to me, that these general strategies apply evenly back to very simple and to the far more complex material of the high school years.

Regarding individual pupils' reading-thinking style, the teacher must consider such things as these. Is the pupil creative? Does he tend to see multiple possibilities in a particular plot line and rank these on a probability basis? Does he simply rattle off wild possibilities without decisions? Is the pupil guarded, cautious, and limited in his thinking to sure bets and certainties? Is he careless, breezy, and heedless of relevant data? Is he close, analytic, and deadly in searching out each conclusion? When uncertainty persists, can he take it; can he maintain an open mind until the data are in? Is he a slave to stereotype and the fixed certainties of his own prior judgments? Has he the will to comprehend and the self-reliance to do so?

Such styles of thinking underpin the reading process. They are its driving force, its engine. No two of us is composed quite alike on these dimensions nor would anyone wish that we were. Yet one can imagine a sort of golden mean among these things that should yield a very powerful reader. More particularly would this be so if this reader knew how to adjust his will, his caution or boldness, his care or his want of it to the necessary circumstances of society and the human needs of his fellows.

The teacher must have some sense of these matters as he directs the reading lesson. If a pupil is bold and insightful, call on him when an important clue to a shift in theme is veiled, so that others may see the effect of his discernment as they read on. There is, of course, no single way to direct any reading lesson with any group of children, but it must involve a purposeful effort on the part of the teacher. Throughout the school years one major purpose of each lesson must be to utilize the intellectual talents of different pupils so that their effects may be examined and evaluated.

My focus so far has been on typical plotted fiction of various sorts. Poetry, myth, song, and stories of classical dimension should not be handled in this scrimmage manner. The goal with this exercise, particularly in the primary and middle school years, must be to see that the students have the *experience* of reading. From this it follows that materials of this kind must be made available in good range and abundance, time to sample them must be provided, and the task shared by teacher and student.

Some years ago I was working with a group of children—fifth graders, I believe—in a demonstration before a gathering of teachers. Each child had previously selected a book he wanted to read. Some had finished; others were at various stages of completion. My plan was to question different children about what they had chosen, and why, and help them assess the degree to which their selection measured up to their expectations. This is a powerful reading strategy and one that should be employed frequently at all grade levels. It allows pupils to examine and learn about real reading that is motivated by taste and natural interests, and it teaches children how to exact standards both of the books they select and themselves.

One child, a rather chubby little boy, brought with him *Charlotte's Web*, which he said he had finished. I asked him casually how he'd happened to pick it, and he replied that he had done so because it was said to be a very good book. My impression at that moment was that he might well be one of those docile children who reads little and just what he is told. I pressed him a bit as to why he would want to read a book like that, whereupon he soon bristled up and said, "They told me it was a good book, and it was." We were all a bit impressed by his warmth.

"Well," I said, "if it *was*, would you find me the part that gave you that impression, that made you know it was?" He agreed to do so, and I turned to work with some other children. In a bit he returned holding about two or three chapters between thumb and forefinger and said, "This part."

"No, Tommy," I said, "that won't do. I want the nugget—something you can read to us in a few minutes." Again he left and didn't return until we were just about to dismiss.

"I've got it," he said, with a look that suggested that he thought I might have forgotten him.

"Good," I said, "Will you read it to us? Use the microphone there."

And so he read in a clear strong voice those incredible lines from *Charlotte's Web* where the carnival is disbanded and Charlotte is dead.

How can I describe it further? We were chilled and hushed and moved by the force of it. A good book had been found, and its merit proved. Everyone of us in the room knew something more about literature and reading and taste and judgment and the power of young minds. If we do not open the door to this kind of language experience often and continually over the years we can scarcely consider that we have taught anything of value at all.

□ Reading the Text

It is almost with a sense of reluctance that I return to the "scrimmage" once again, but if this feeling on my part points up the difference between *reading* and *reading lessons* and the superordinate importance of the former, then my plan was well conceived. Nonetheless, all reading that we do is not classics, nor is it storybook fiction. An important part of the corpus is that of the substantive disciplines—mathematics, science, social science. Skillfulness in dealing with these works, too, is demanded of every student.

A variation of the directed reading-thinking activity is needed in order to deal with works of this kind. As will be recalled, the principal probe questions of the teacher directing the reading of a story are

"How do you think the story will go? What will it be about? What will happen next?" Questions of this kind are not useful in the reading of science. Many a college freshman has foundered from the tacit but altogether false belief that if he has deduced what the text was about, his reading assignment is finished.

In works of this kind, the text is organized, not on the logic of life, but on an abstract logic which itself is the inner structure and theoretical plan of the discipline itself. Thus biology, in one rendering at least, may be thought to reflect Darwinian theory, from which derives a linear, topological mapping of creatures whose attributes are significant as they differentiate one from another and advance progressively across the millenia. In a textbook dealing with this topic, what is said, where, and when is governed by this underlying structure. What the student of this text must learn is not only that the chapter is about cephalopods and their characteristics but also the relevance of these characteristics to the biological frame. Moreover, unless one were gifted with photographic memory, the learning of those vast numbers of differentiating characteristics would soon prove overwhelming. It is by the application of the frame that one form of life predicts another so that the new may be added to the old in a comfortable, assimilable manner.

At an early age, children can begin to learn the characteristics of different kinds of textual writing and the self-discipline that study reading requires. As with other lessons in reading this one too needs repeated exercise upward through the grades as new dimensions of reasoning become viable and new areas of study are encountered.

The change of teaching techniques for material of this kind is relatively simple. First, the teacher directs the children to find out what the article will be about. They must start with this as a given. They do so by noting the title, skimming the text, and observing the illustrations or diagrams. Next, the teacher provides those lead questions which his knowledge of the underlying frame suggests are fruitful for this particular passage.

If the topic is the making of butter, speculation might be directed toward these questions: "What does butter come from? How then *is* it made? What are its uses?" Simple though these may seem, when second graders are pressed to think things through (and it is the teacher's responsibility to see that they do), they will come up with a fascinating mixture of magic and fact that will set them squarely on target for the reading task. The teacher, of course, does not supply the answers but requires only that they do their own best serious thinking.

Now when the children read, the objective is to confirm or reject these previous judgments and to flesh out what is known with what is new. Following the silent reading, the teacher determines how thoroughly this has been done by returning to the original leading questions. At this point the pupils are held to the highest standard of response that the text itself can support. This may require rereading, rethinking, vocabulary study; and the task is not complete, i.e., study reading has not been accomplished, until all that can be is in fact done.

From this example perhaps you can see why I think it so very important that material of this kind be well written and truly informative. A mish-mash of facts in a "cutesy" setting is simply unmanageable for serious instructional purposes.

As children are exercised in tasks of this kind, they gradually assimilate the questioning bases that underlie different kinds of articles and subject matter areas. They also learn how to vary their rate of reading in relation to their prior knowledge of the field. They gain further an increasingly informed sense of vocabulary—they learn when new terms and new concepts must be forged and how this is done through reading. They learn when and how to use graphs and charts, pictures, glossaries, and dictionaries. These critical understandings, so often presented in isolated skills books, are best learned here in the heat of study reading that is held to a rigorous standard.

Perhaps the most commonly known prescription for teaching teenagers to study is Robinson's SQ3R formula (1961)—survey, question, read, recite, review. It is a good one, and as you can see, something of this order underlies the strategy I have proposed. Unfortunately, however, if a pupil's expectations and disciplines have not been built in advance, the Robinson formula will avail him nothing. He has not the underlying knowledge to ask the question even if he does make a survey. Further, he will lack that standard of rigor to which the question must be taken if it is to serve a study purpose. This I think is why most presetting study devices (Ausubel organizers [1960] or plans derived from frame theory) have so little effectiveness.

As children advance to new disciplines and materials of greater complexity, it is important that "subject matter" teachers understand the kind of language-learning experiences that are required by their texts. Where deficiencies exist, they must be dealt with then by that teacher in the context of his course. A few side trips to a well-run reading laboratory may help, but the educational objective cannot be reached if subject matter teachers set standards that are beyond or beneath their pupils' reach.

☐ Word Study

Like the advancing power of young readers to comprehend what their interests and duties call them to, so does their knowledge of word advance gradually across the years in a smooth and natural interaction with their total language experience. As with all else in this enterprise, the surface of language is the source upon which this knowledge feeds, but it does so only as it can and as it is exercised to do so. It is for this reason that sight words for reading may not be thrust in from outside; it is only as they are acquired in the context of written language that they will attain that permanence of residency in the mind from which successive levels of phonological knowledge may be derived. This is true also of new concepts and the spoken and written labels that denote them. It is for this reason that isolated vocabulary drill is so notoriously ineffective as a teaching device.

To master the literate world, children must actively engage their wills to comprehend. They must groom their intellectual capacities ever more efficiently to the task, and they must embrace those standards of rigor that comport with those capacities. The directed reading-thinking activities described above are teaching strategies designed to effect these ends. While doubtless there are other ways, I think them good and see them as the primary pedagogical devices for promoting vocabulary development. If, however, the curriculum does not extend beyond this point to exercise taste and selection in reading and curiosity and commitment to the substantive disciplines, these exercises alone will be quite insufficient. To reverse the old saw, "Every teacher must be a teacher of reading," I suggest that every teacher of reading must be committed to the wonders of the world and all the disciplines that define them.

Word knowledge then comes from this source and so, in the more narrow sense, does orthographic knowledge, for, as we have seen, this depends on semantic and syntactic principles as well as on those of phonology. The program of word study that I recommend undertakes to build on this resource progressively. Children's reading and writing provide continuous information about what they may be ready to explore. The manner in which I lead them to do so becomes gradually less formalized as they move upward through the middle school. When, however, children reach that point at which they can think maturely about their language, I suggest that they should study not simply words, but language itself in its many facets. If we wish to have informed parents and teachers in the future, it is here that such learning should begin.

I left word study, in the preceding section on early reading instruction, with children who were fairly well established as spellers of known words in what we have been calling the transitional phase. The examples in Chart 2, again from Gentry (1977a), will remind you of the characteristics of this phase.

The bench marks of this transitional stage are the generally accurate use of short vowels in simple accented closed syllables, the presence of a vowel in unaccented syllables, presence of preconsonantal nasals, and the presence of, but frequent inaccuracies with, vowel markers (as in the silent e in *lame* or silent a in *soap*).

When pupils reach this stage, I continue to have them sort words by number of syllables, beginning consonant elements, short vowel patterns, and such aspects of meaning as occurs to them or that I think they can deal with. These sorts are done either with word-bank words, or, if the bank has been put aside, as it usually is by this time, I use packets or small boxes of word chips that I have reason to think most

Chart 2. Invented Spellings by Four Children at Progressive Stages of
Orthographic Knowledge

KEY	STAGE 1 PREPHONETIC	STAGE 2 PHONETIC	STAGE 3 TRANSITIONAL	STAGE 4 ADVANCED
monster	m	MOSTR	MONSTRE	MONSTER
united		UNINT	UNINTIDE	UNITED
dressing	s	GASIN	JRAISING	DREESING
bottom	b	BODM	BODOME	BOTTOM
hiked	h	HIT	HICKTE	HIKED
human	m	HUMN	HUMUNE	HUMAN
eagle	e	EGO	EGLLE	EGLE
closed	c	COST	KLOSDE	CLOSED
number	m	NOMR	NOMBER	NUMBER
peeked	p	PET	PEPTE	PEAKED
sink	s	SEC	SINKCE	SINK
bumpy	b	BOPE	BOMPE	BUMPY

will be able to identify. These activities consolidate the known. Formal
instruction presses forward to the new.

Long Vowel Patterns

The errors that children make at the stage we have labeled "Vowel
Transition" show that they know at a tacit level that in English spelling
the value of the vowel (long or short) is signaled by the pattern. We
infer this from the fact that they include markers when they wish to
spell a long vowel. This state of knowledge is the signal to us as teachers that they are now ready to examine these patterns in detail and
make what they know more accurate and, as need be, explicit.

The goal of our instruction is not to make of our pupils little linguists—either psycho- or historical. But we most certainly do intend
that they develop a habit of examining the spelling patterns of English
and relating each to particular word meanings. These patterns are historically derived; they are reasonably limited in number; they have
psychological utility; and they can be learned. More importantly,
what must be learned beyond this point depends on a sound functional mastery of this characteristic of English words.

Throughout this work I have argued that there is "method to the
madness" of English spelling (Vallins 1973). It can be derived logically
from the surface (Venezky 1967). It can be derived phonologically
(Chomsky and Halle 1968) and historically (Scragg 1974; Bradley
1918). Finally, we have shown that children have a natural propensity
to respond to and build toward this logic. The business of education
is to cultivate this remarkable talent.

Consider again the progression of word knowledge. We have seen that before children know what a word is they cannot segment it or remember it. When they know what words are they can do both. Yet their ability at first to store words in memory is rather fragile. Initially their words are composed of a kind of frame in which letters march from left to right. Sometimes words are arrayed as children expect (one letter/one sound), sometimes not, and that is why remembering them at this stage is more difficult than it will be later on. At the letter-name stage it is fruitless to teach vowel patterns; just as it was fruitless to teach phoneme segmentation before a word concept was formed. But once the pattern concept is tacitly grasped, then children can learn specific vowel patterns and learn to relate them to meaning.

Initially it is sufficient to call children's attention explicitly to the particular patterns of each long vowel. Their normal speaking-reading vocabulary will bring them in contact with the high frequency forms, and these will contrast memorably with those that are less usual. Frequently occurring long *a* patterns are these: *a*, consonant and silent *e*; *a*, silent *i*, consonant; or *a*, silent *y*, blank (the *y* for *i* substitution is as old as the language and has been met often by children at this point). Less common patterns are *eigh*, *ea*, *ei*, and *ey*. Children need to be attuned to these sequences. Notice that seemingly anomolous words like *they*, *grey*, and *fey* are as consistent as the *ai* to *ay* variations in the more common pattern.

By degrees, homonyms enter children's sight vocabulary. Armed with the ability to examine patterns structurally they will then find these visually distinct forms memorable. Moreover, it is this pattern-to-meaning relationship that supports the logic and power of English orthography. Consider the homonyms *vane*, *vain*, and *vein*. The first comes from Old English *fana*, which leads by another route to *banner*. *Vain*, *vanity*, *vacuum*—empty pride, puffed up like a toad—from Latin *vanus* (empty). *Vein*, a blood vessel from Latin *vena* (venial sin, human and pardonable). In each case there is a different pattern, a different meaning, and a different derivation. Further, these distinctions are maintained orthographically in the forms derived from each.

It is important to recognize at this point that English spelling *does* require memorization. We spell *steak* we eat with the pattern *eak*. We

Chart 3. Spelling Patterns of Long A in English Words

able	vacation	
vane	grate	stake
way	play	
vain	rain	
great	steak	
vein	feint	
weigh	reign	
they	grey	

spell *stake* we drive in the ground with the pattern *ake*. They must be differentiated and remembered. But once this is done their forms extend consistently and efficiently into the larger vocabulary of adulthood. In addition, there is often direct information phonetically across exemplars of a given root. This can be seen and heard in the pairs: *vein-venial, vain-vanity.*

When confronted by a vowel chart showing all the different patterns for all the different vowels, one is inclined to throw up one's hands and say, "This is impossible." When to this is added the many consonant variations (*sugar, school, science, scene*), and silent letters (*bomb, cough, knight,* and *psyche*), it is understandable that language historians should have concluded that English spelling is *bad* (Baugh 1957) and that many should have sought to reform it.

As we have seen, all efforts toward phonetic reform have been rejected for 500 years. This alone might lead one to suspect that there is some greater utility in the system as it has evolved. I am persuaded that there is. More importantly, we have found that children from the beginning are disposed toward these abstractions. My contention therefore is that we need pedagogically to do three things: (1) limit our standard of correctness to a level consistent with children's language experience; (2) see to it that the pattern-to-meaning-to-derivation system is in fact examined by children as their vocabulary affords it; and (3) avoid, by act or word, the implication that English is impossible to learn to spell. Many respond to its ordering with no formal instruction at all. To explore its ways is fascinating and by doing so, most will learn to be accurate readers and spellers.

With advanced pupils in grade one, Betty Lee teaches the common long vowel patterns at reading circle and individually by drawing on the children's word banks. She follows this up by giving them simple exercises in spelling to pattern: "Spell these *ain* words—*rain, train, drain, main*," etc. By grade two or beyond a formal study sequence can be set up which is prepared for by pre-teaching at circle and practiced as a group at each student's seat. Individual work stations are signaled by a 3" × 5" card on which key words for particular vowels are printed. Attached to the cards are a set of envelopes containing word chips to be sorted according to the key patterns.

An important feature of this sorting task is that it contains, in addition to the targeted or keyed patterns, a miscellaneous column. Into this column go words that look as though they should fit the categories but for some reason do not. At an early stage, words like *have, come,* and *love* are likely candidates for the miscellaneous column. Exemplars falling in this category can often be explained logically and so generate new word categories or spelling conventions.

In these sorting tasks, of course, the teacher controls the variability because she picks the words that go into the envelopes. It is generally best to start with simple exemplars and work toward more complex ones. By degrees both short and long vowel patterns are combined, and patterns arrayed across vowels. This same plan may be followed for introducing the *r*-influenced patterns, which can really be done earlier than is found in most programs because there are many such words in a primary reading vocabulary.

The foregoing tasks are closed, that is, the teacher picks the exemplars. These closed tasks are matched with open tasks which we sometimes call "Word Hunts." In word hunts a 5" × 8" card again signals the categories, including a miscellaneous column. Directions advise pupils to find exemplars and write them in columns on their work paper. Pupils may be directed to hunt in their readers, or storybooks, in magazines or newspapers. They may also simply "think of words they know." The territory for hunting may be defined as the teacher wishes.

With these tasks it is wise to check the pupils' work with them, and then to save it in folders as a record of progress. Children who can gather a suitable set of exemplars in a limited period of search *know* how to discriminate words by their vowel patterns.

Consonants

Vowels are not the only source of perplexity and misspelling in English, though they account for most of it. Consonants, too, have varied patterns. The letters and letter digraphs *s*, *sh*, *ch*, *sk*, *sl* serve a varied lot of sounds and are much bemoaned by those who would reform our language. My approach to these matters is to accept, group, and note them as exemplars accrue in children's working vocabularies. The basic patterns are familiar and easily learned: /tʃ/ = *ch* in *chin*; /ʃ/ = *sh* in *shoe*; /s/ = *s* in *sent*; /s/ = *c* in *cent*, and so on. Children meet these forms early in their writing and master them easily. Later they must work out hard *c* as in *cart* and *cat*; and final /k/ as in *back* and *bake* and *music*; also *g* in *goat*, *get* and *gym*. It is seldom worth the time to bother with *s* as /s/ /z/ in *cats* and *dogs*, or with /ð/ and /θ/ as *th* in *than* and *thing*. These patterns seem easily grasped without instruction.

Curiously, children are less troubled by silent consonants than the language reformers would have us think. Doubtless the novelty of the form makes them memorable. I think it useful, however, to talk about such words—explaining the lost aspirates *k* and *gh* and the vestigial *b* in *bomb* from *bombard*. The reason for this is to give assurance that our spelling system is not just phonetic, but derivational as well. (Nor would I hesitate to point out some true anomalies like *ghost* and *island* in which silent letters came in by analogy and false derivation. Our system at best is optimal, not perfect.)

The more interesting variations (and the more troublesome for the uninstructed speller) come about in the lower frequency words. To deal with these, children must learn how to examine polysyllabic words and how to deal with affixes (prefixes, suffixes, and inflectional endings). The key to all of this is the structural principle of the open and closed syllables.

Recently I examined a spelling sample drawn from a fourth grade class. The words *stopped*, *fanning*, *taming*, and *forgetting* were troublesome for nearly everyone, yet the children could spell *prop* and *ban* and *lame* and *forget* without difficulty. What they did not know was that the structural pattern that applies to long and short vowels is carried over to words of more than one syllable and when inflections are added.

The principle is quite simple. A short vowel holds the pattern intact by doubling or adding a silent consonant. When this is not done, the syllable falls "open" and the vowel becomes long. Thus to go from *fan* to *fanning* the consonant *n* must double, or else it would read *fā ning*. Accordingly, when *tame* adds an *ing*, the *e* is dropped; the first syllable opens, and the vowel remains long—*tā ming*. (Never mind where the hyphen goes or how the word is divided in the dictionary—this is the way the principle works.) Children must be walked through the patterns until they can do them automatically. To accomplish this end both closed and open sort tasks and spelling drills are appropriate.

Consider the pattern as it works for affixing. If *er* is added, *stop* becomes *stopper*, and *tame* becomes *tamer*. If *less* is added, *hat* becomes *hatless* and *home* becomes *homeless*. *Hat* is closed and remains so with the simple addition of *less*; *home* must preserve its *e* marker since without it the word would read *hŏm less*.

In most phonics books, common syllable patterns are labeled VC/CV, e.g., *basket*; +*Cle*, e.g., *table*, *cattle*; V/CV; VC/V, e.g., *pilot*, *robin*. Syllable rules are not of much use to a reader, but for the speller who already can pronounce the word, the consonant doubling principle is most helpful. Sound will guide him where to divide the word and illuminate what must be remembered.

Consider the examples above. *Basket* has two syllables; the first is stressed, the vowel is short, and the syllable is closed. There is nothing to "remember"; its correct spelling is automatic. With *table* and *cattle*, the open syllable and closed syllable with silent consonant are similarly automatic. All that must be remembered here is the common *le* form for vocalic L, or /əl/, as some dictionaries list it.

Now examine *pilot* and *robin*. Sound tells you that the first syllable of *pilot* is *pi* and the first syllable of *robin* is *rob*. By principle they have to be that way. But one might justifiably expect the *b* in *robin* to double. It does not. It is anomalous and must be remembered as such. When the habit of examining words and making sense of them is established, then curiosities are easily dealt with. Observe next an Old French borrowing from medieval Latin, *mińute*. The first syllable is just as expected. The second is unstressed and not spelled as it sounds. If at this point a helpful teacher points out the root *minūtus* = small, and the other English word and homograph, *minuté*, the mystery will dissolve under the light of meaning, and another valuable spelling principle will have been experienced.

The principle of consonant doubling cannot be too thoroughly ingrained. Our teaching failure in the past has been to talk about it vaguely and pass on, but it is a beachhead that must be occupied and held.

For vowel patterns and common variable consonant patterns and for syllable principles I use and recommend a formal sequence of instruction. There should be direct instruction and supervised practice. Thereafter, assigned individual practice of the kind described in the open and closed sort tasks should be maintained until those understandings are mastered and automatic.

From the beginning, however, there should be frequent word-study activities derived from the vocabulary follow-up after reading and during the weekly writing critique. At each such session, words that are new, perplexing, or simply interesting should be examined. At these meetings the teacher should be equipped with a good college-level dictionary. My practice is to have children as a group speculate about the words—think of analogous words, derivations, and the like. Then I consult the dictionary, and we resolve the issue together. There is no substitute for the teacher's demonstrating dictionary use by using it himself for the group purpose. This general format of group word study is a useful one to follow upward through the grades as the more elaborate vocabulary of these years is met and examined.

Derivations and Classic Roots

As we have seen over and over again, it is the convention of English spelling to preserve meaning units (be they roots or affixes) across sound changes. Children meet this phenomenon early in grade one. Initially they spell the past tense inflection *ed*, as *t*, *d*, or vowel plus *d*, just as they hear it phonetically. Usually within a year the constant form *ed* is applied across its changes of sound, and so silently does this knowledge steal upon them that many adults are quite unaware of the varied sounds that *ed* actually represents. Probably the same is true for most of the regular patterns that control the accuracy of the natural good speller. When, however, the less-gifted speller experiences uncertainty, doubt, and fear, he behaves "childishly"—he reverts to spelling by sound. It is for this reason that I advocate that word study be continued upward through the grades, that word patterns be learned, their behaviors observed, and their dividends garnered.

Many times derivational evidence is not immediately useful. The fact that in Old English words ending with /s/ were spelled *s* as in *mouse* is interesting. Some may be amused to learn it was the Normans who changed our plural form from *mys* to *mice* and *is* to *ice* (Vallins 1973), and that *c* after *i* is now a convention. But this does not save the beginner from memorizing *dance* and *fence* and *face* versus *case* and *horse*. For good reason one develops a sort of feel for this task, but certainly not at a tender age. As Templeton (1980) has noted, however, explorations of this kind do serve as a helpful mnemonic, particularly with older children. As an aid to our pedagogical memory, he further points out that the silent *m* in *mnemonic* may be heard when the same root is used in the words *anmesty* and *amnesia!* One of my favorites of this kind is the seemingly innocent word *helicopter*—a happy compound from the Greek *helix* (spiral) and *pter* (wing). When fourth graders confront me with their collection of prehistoric animals, I am ready to inform them about the noble *pterodactyl*.

To conclude this section, I have gathered some sets of word pairs which suggest conventions that aid correct spelling in various ways. Frith (1980) has pointed out that there are exceptions to these patterns. Indeed there are, but by examining them pupils will gain confidence in the usefulness of "looking with a plan." Such observation makes exceptions memorable.

The regularities revealed in these groupings are dictated by derivations. Were we or our students competent Latinists, the system and the exceptions would be quite obvious. Even so, this want of education is not a bar to our noting certain consistencies and developing a "feel" for the way these words are spelled. One should be cautious, however, of attempting to formalize such observations into *rules*. Leave that to the philologist.

It is sufficient to play along the surface of things, forming rough principles and checking these out against the dictionary entry. Consider the *tion/sion* variation, for example. On the surface it seems that *ide, ode, ude, ell, se, ss, rt* take *sion* while *ite, ate, ce* and so on take *tion*. Let's make it simpler: *de, se* take *sion; ce, te* take *tion*. This will give us *persuade/persuasion; induce/induction*. Very good. If *contend* changes to *contention*, why is *intension* spelled *sion*? As the dictionary will show, the latter pairs with *intense*, like *suspense* and *suspension*, while *intend* like *contend* yields *intention*. So there is some

Chart 4. Word Ending -tion -sion

-sion	-tion
divide–division	ignite–ignition
invade–invasion	invite–invitation
explode–explosion	incubate–incubation
include–inclusion	alternate–alternation
expel–expulsion	inflate–inflation
compel–compulsion	reduce–reduction
express–expression	produce–production
confess–confession	invent–invention
admit–admission	retain–retention
commit–commission	receive–reception
divert–diversion	deceive–deception
convert–conversion	inscribe–inscription

Chart 5. Words Ending -ible -able

-able	-ible
attainable	compressible
salable	impossible
inflammable	accessible
probable	apprehensible
invariable	defensible
measurable	deducible
accountable	reducible
receivable	convertible
reliable	controvertible
respectable	reversible
definable	invincible

Chart 6. Words Pairs Showing Vowel Alternation and Vowel Reduction

Vowel alternation	Vowel reduction
sane–sanity	restore–restoration
serene–serenity	photograph–photography
malign–malignity	competent–compete
declare–declaration	consolation–console
inspire–inspiration	immigrate–migration
decide–decision	history–historical
convene–convention	manager–managerial
resign–resignation	preservation–preserve
divide–division	resolute–resolution
nation–national	introduction–introduce
incline–inclination	medicine–medicinal

method to this madness, and it is one that will steal upon us if we let it.

A similar analysis will help to clarify the old spelling problem of the endings *ible* and *able*. It is some comfort to find that the pattern is like that already found for *tion*. The root *vis* in *revise* yields *sion* in *revision* and *ible* in *visible*. So we may hope to slay a common college spelling demon.

Pupils should also be encouraged to observe the alteration and reduction of the vowel elements as inflections are added. They will find that unstressed vowels and silent consonants, held constant in spelling, appear on the surface as the stress pattern shifts across these different forms. These conventions support both the speller and the reader who would be in a sorry plight indeed if our words were rendered each by phonetic transcription /kəneidian/ /kænɔdɔ/ (Bradley 1918).

Conclusion

When a teacher writes about teaching, the principal problem for the reader is the fear that he will never stop. Pupils, with considerable justification, have a similar difficulty with our talking. Accordingly, I will bring this chapter to a close with unusual and wholly unprofessional brevity.

Our research began because I felt altogether uncertain about what children knew about words as they learned to read and spell. What we have found has shed a good deal of light on this issue. I have tried to show in this chapter that I am now able to compose instructional procedures that work in harmony with this developmental progression and do so in a comprehensive way that shows an equal concern for competence and performance. Needless to say it is my hope that teachers will find these ideas useful in building programs of their own.

It may seem overambitious to treat a subject so large and complex as reading disability in a concluding chapter of a work of this kind. I undertake it because I believe that we can learn much about what should go on in the teaching of reading by a careful study of what, from time to time, has gone wrong. Also I have come to feel that our studies of children's progressive word knowledge offer some relatively new and powerful insights for the diagnostician. These I want to share. Finally, I am aware that concern for reading and writing failure runs high, and I believe this concern is justified. I do not think, however, that hasty efforts for "early detection" and mass remediation will solve our problems. Instead I think that an analysis of reading disability suggests the need for deliberate and long-range actions by parents, administrators, reading teachers, special educators, and classroom teachers. My conclusion will undertake to declare these varied roles as I see them serving us best. I end with the plea that we approach this task soberly, seriously, and confidently.

What is Dyslexia?

No reading teacher can escape this question. It comes at him at parties and in the grocery store, at school and at play, and even in the home after the Thanksgiving feast. Unfortunately, so many answers have been given to the question, by educators of diverse opinions, by substantive scholars differently over the years, by newspaper writers interpreting the topic as best they can, that any answer is bound to conflict with what has been said before. It is a bit like interpreting scripture. As a consequence, many of my colleagues would prefer that the word not be used at all.

For my part I think dyslexia, as a clinical classification, is both legitimate and useful, provided that reasonable care is employed in its application. My first meeting with the term was in the work of Knud Hermann (Hermann and Norrie 1958), the Danish neurologist who argued that in the absence of specific brain injury a pattern of clinical behaviors similar to those evidenced by Gerstmann syndrome should justify the assumption that a common malfunction of the central nervous system underlay each. Where lesions were known to exist he used the label alexia. Where diagnosis was reached on the basis of clinical features, he used the label dyslexia. So defined, the conditions delimiting a diagnosis of dyslexia are fairly clear. There must first be a recognized brain pathology with documented clinical characteristics. Only then may these serve as the basis for inference about an underlying central cause of reading difficulty.

Geschwind's writings (1974) illuminate both the complexity and some of the verities that appear to hold between language function and the brain. He notes in one article that Hermann's focus upon Gerstmann's syndrome was too narrow in that there clearly are other patterns of lesion that result in reading failure. Specifically, damage to the dominant visual interpretative area plus damage to the corpus callosum, by which information from the right visual area must pass to the dominant language center, do lead to a complete inability to read. In addition he shows that the dominant clinical feature of Gerstmann's syndrome is a breakdown in writing (agraphia) and not necessarily in reading at all.

A second very real difficulty in this use of the term dyslexia lies in the fact that one cannot translate directly from patterns of lesion and their attendant clinical features for adults to surface sets of conditions among young children. In youth, central function is more plastic. The dominant hemisphere of a child, for example, may be excised, and language will continue to advance normally, whereas a similar ablation at maturity will destroy language altogether and permanently. In addition, the fact of having already learned to speak, read, and write may well alter the clinical picture vis-à-vis one who has not yet accomplished this task. Thus, among adults suffering from a memory disorder that obscures the recent past, language may remain intact. For children, however, whose language learning falls under the shadow of nonrecall, loss of language may well be entailed.

The classic aphasic conditions stemming from injury to Broca's area, Wernicke's area, or the relational system between these and other areas of memory and motor response appear regularly to interfere with reading and writing. It is also possible to identify specific deficits in reading or writing, and in reading and writing, without a concomitant deficit in oral language production or comprehension. In my experience, conditions of this kind present themselves quite explicitly in clinical terms, some of which I will illustrate presently. Gerstmann's syndrome, with its clinical features of dyscalcula, agraphia, finger agnosia, and orientation disability simply does exist, for me, not only in the literature but in the attributes of a life-long friend. This classic brain damage syndrome too is real with its well-described features of lability, compulsivity, hyperactivity, and aberrations perceptually and conceptually in figure-ground and object association tasks. Children presenting these characteristics have enormous difficulty learning to read and write.

It must be emphasized, however, that these syndromes of primary reading-writing disability are rare. When the clinical picture is un-ambiguous and there is reasonable evidence to support the belief that brain injury has occurred, I am content to apply the diagnostic label alexia. Where there is no evidence of trauma but clinical signs are clear, I think it reasonable to infer a congenital difficulty and to label such cases dyslexic. Where conditions *are* ambiguous, a far more cautious approach to diagnostic labeling should be taken. A brief review of the procedures that I have come to follow will be given shortly. Before doing so, however, I feel impelled to deal with the "broadcast" use of the term dyslexia and its euphemistic cousin, "learning disability," for which I have considerable misgivings.

The Learning Disability Issue

The present widely used term "learning disability," or *LD*, is a substitute for the more alarming label, "minimal brain damaged," or *MBD*. Its cloaked synonymity may be discerned in such statements as "These children *have* LD (rather than *are* MBD)." With the adoption of this new term and its legitimization by federal funding (Carrier 1977), the criterion for diagnosis became "anyone reading below grade level." Thus we are asked to believe that all programs of reading instruction and all conditions of man are optimal and that any who fall by the wayside must do so from modest if not colossal impairment of the brain. Such a posture seems to me altogether unreasonable and dangerously misleading.

The origins of the learning disability syndrome do have some scientific integrity. They began with the work of Strauss (1955) who applied the clinical features of brain damage to the study of the mentally retarded. By so doing, he succeeded in discriminating between exogenous and endogenous conditions. Cruickshank's work (1961) was developed from this research base. He advanced pedagogical procedures (largely a systematic reduction of distracting stimulation) to a population of children who presented similar clinical features to those of Strauss's mental retardates.

The work of Kirk (1971), Kephart (1971), Frostig and Horne (1964), and others has centered upon the perceptual features of this brain-damaged syndrome. By extension and extrapolation to "normal" populations, they have sought to infer minimal brain damage on the basis of performance on tests of perceptual function.

While one must take the work of these scholars seriously and applaud both their ingenuity and sincerity, difficulty lies in the way of any blanket application of these constructs to reading disability as a whole. It is simply a fact that not all dyslexics and most certainly not all disabled readers suffer from hyperactivity and/or figure-ground confusion. The application of systematic stimulus control to all children who are "behind in reading" is not justified. Similarly, perceptual test batteries built on an abstract psychological model (e.g., the Illinois Test of Psycholinguistic Abilities [ITPA]; see Paraskevopoulos and Kirk 1969) are far removed indeed from the physiological base that they imply (Carroll 1972). Many able readers fare badly on such instruments, and the opposite is equally true. Moreover, the internal and predictive validity of the best of these psychometric tools has met serious challenge (Hammill et al. 1974; Hammill and Larsen 1974). The clouds of correlational data derived from this line of research are not only complex and confusing (see Bannatyne 1971); they are palpably unconvincing. One does not doubt that reading involves perception or that certain syndromes of reading disability may turn upon a perceptual deficit. In my experience, some do. What I here question is the capability of any single instrument to predict, let alone to serve as the basis for correction of all problems in learning to read. It is naive and beyond reason to expect that this should be the case.

That one may be disabled as a learner is all too common knowledge, but not all who suffer this condition are abnormal. Unfortunately, language-related injuries do happen to some children, and other children very probably do suffer a congenital impairment of the central nervous system. Beyond this point, however, one must expect and anticipate variation in aptitude within, above, and below the "normal" range. The responsibility of educators and the communities that employ them is to meet these varied capacities. If such normal children fail, it is the system that has failed, and there can be little profit in asserting abnormality of the children as an excuse.

Geschwind (1974) speaks directly to this point as he considers "disorders of higher cortical function in children." I think there can be no doubt that we share a common view of what is normal and what is not.

> Let me turn away briefly from the acquired disorders of childhood to that whole array of so-called developmental disorders. I think that to treat all of these special learning deficits as abnormalities is probably incorrect in most instances, and that most of these children are normal variants of the human species. One must remember that practically all of us have a significant number of special learning disabilities. In most cases these disabilities do not get us into difficulties, but this is merely cultural accident. For example, I am grossly unmusical and cannot carry a tune. A significant number of children are unmusical despite valiant attempts to teach them, while others are obviously highly endowed despite total lack of any special instruction. Some children similarly are very artistic and can draw beautifully, and others, like myself, are quite incapable of drawing even reasonably. Such difficulties are quite widespread throughout the human race, yet we, the unmusical minority and the unartistic majority, are not labelled as suf-

fering from "minimal brain dysfunction." As in most species of animals, talents are distributed asymmetrically. We happen to live in a society in which the child who has trouble learning to read is in difficulty. Yet we have all seen some dyslexic children who draw much better than controls, *i.e.*, who have either superior visual perception or visual motor skills. My suspicion would be that in an illiterate society such a child would be in little difficulty and might in fact do better because of his superior visual-perceptual talents, while many of us who function well here might do poorly in a society in which a quite different array of talents was needed to be successful. In most cases, we probably are not talking about disease but about children who have run up against the demands of this society for particular sets of talents. As the demands of society change, will we acquire a new group of "minimally brain-damaged"? (p. 479)

Diagnosis of Reading Disabilities

☐ Rationale

Diagnosis of reading/writing disabilities is a work achieved by a diagnostician; it cannot be managed blindly by the application of standard tests. Clinicians must be apprised of the literature on disability as well as that of normal language development and reading, and they must be competent in test administration, interviewing techniques, and the like. More than this, however, they must have an extended and guided experience with specific cases of disabled readers so that they can achieve a well-integrated sense of the conditions that influence learning of typical cases against which to view each new and necessarily unique client. They must learn to proceed with an open mind, moving cautiously from hypothesis to hypothesis as they discern relationships among the data until reasonable sense can be made of a particular child's condition. Diagnosis must never end with a label but always with a working plan of action to be taken socially, emotionally, and pedagogically.

Because I view diagnosis in this manner, I am convinced that a year-long practicum should be required for all reading specialists. This work should be carried on under the direct supervision of an experienced clinician who can show by example both the techniques and the exercise of judgment that are needed. No formula will suffice nor will practice by a teacher alone convey what must be mastered. These same conditions hold, it should be added, for remedial instruction as well. It is only by experiencing the effects of refined teaching that students learning to be teachers are gradually able to free themselves from the false belief that it is the method rather than they themselves that must control the set for learning.

There is much silly talk today about diagnostic-prescriptive teaching which in operation proceeds in a sequence of "test-teach-test." Nothing, I think, could be more simplistic or less fitting as a means of dealing with a human learner. Such programs, quite like token systems of reward, are altogether wanting in the sensitivity, speed, and accuracy that fine teaching requires. Truly diagnostic-prescriptive teaching can occur only as it flows all-of-a-piece from within the teacher. Rewards there are, both positive and negative, but these must be delivered naturally and precisely by posture, eye, voice tone, and direct assertion. Such teaching skill is learned only gradually, by example and practice. Reading specialists who have attained this level of understanding and self-control are thereby able to help all teachers in normal developmental classrooms. They are not just specialists with a bag of tricks and labels. It is thus that our investment of interest in diagnosis and remediation focuses not simply on the disabled but on sound teaching at large and the *prevention* of learning disabilities.

☐ Diagnostic Procedures

At our Center, the diagnostic procedure advances in this way. The child and his parents arrive by appointment at about ten o'clock, at which time an individual test of intelligence, or the so-called "psychological," is administered. This is given by a psychometrician who is fully acquainted with our testing program. The child's application contains only a bare minimum of information, name, age, and the like, so that each examiner has an opportunity to meet the child with a fully open mind.

After the individual intelligence test has been completed, the child goes to lunch with his parents and returns at one o'clock to meet and begin work with a reading diagnostician. At this same time his parents meet with another examiner who on this and the following day will conduct two scheduled interviews covering the child's history and his present-day social-emotional climate.

In the reading diagnosis we begin with a brief interview and then turn directly to informal tests of word-recognition, reading, spelling, and writing. Our materials follow quite closely those described by Emmett Betts some thirty years ago (1946), though they are based on a contemporary set of readers. In this test battery, the child is exposed to word lists drawn from the readers and to passages which he reads aloud and silently. Comprehension is measured by prepared questions which the examiner delivers orally. Spelling is tested directly by graded lists, and writing or dictation is elicited in relation to some appropriate stimulus activity. Some explanation perhaps is needed to justify our use of such an old-fashioned method of reading evaluation.

☐ Why Informal Inventories are Used

There are a good number of formalized or semi-standardized informal inventories on the market. I do not like any of them. In some, the passages don't suit me; in others, the comprehension questions are uninteresting or frankly faulty, and in all of them there is the "full-face" implication that the scores are valid and meaningful in and of themselves. The value and power of informal testing, as I see it, is to present the child with school-like material and observe how he deals with it. The scores a child may attain are almost incidental to the rich complex of observational data that such a procedure provides. This concept, however, is one of the very most difficult to convey to teaching students. It has been my experience that students are far more receptive to keeping the test in its place when it is one that they have helped to construct or revise. They then know its frailties and thus are more easily persuaded to keep their eyes and mind on the child.

Many may also wonder why I have not adopted the analysis of oral reading miscues (*Goodman Miscue Analysis*) (Goodman and Burke 1972). I do demonstrate this highly refined instrument for students and have them study the scoring system carefully. When, however, a sensitivity to dialect and the power of meaningful insertions is gained, I feel this may be applied quite adequately to the old-fashioned reading inventory. In addition, I have some qualms about an overvaluation of word identification that is meaningful but in fact wrong. Some miscues are interesting and do suggest that the reader is using his head, but any rendition that must be so labored through is functionally unsatisfactory as reading, regardless of the adequacy of the pupils' comprehension.

Finally, one may wonder why it is that I use a list of ten questions to test comprehension when I am so opposed to this technique as a teaching device. The fact is that I think such questions, if skillfully written and *carefully probed*, make an excellent and highly efficient informal testing device. In my opinion, asking a student to recall, in his own words, what he read is sloppy and time wasting by comparison.

☐ Informal Testing Continued

When, as often happens with young children, their word knowledge is too meager for them to read at all, we proceed with informal readiness screening in much the same fashion as a good first-grade teacher would. An excellent informal instrument has been composed by one of our students, Donald Bear. It includes figure identification, letter- and word-matching tasks, invented spelling and writing, dictation and supported reading measures for concept of word and sight acquisition. It concludes with the child's selecting a good story that we read to him in full. Few tests are as informative and none so pleasant to give.

With regard to spelling and writing, we are now able to make a fairly accurate accounting of the child's knowledge of English words. We can specify the approximate grade level or frequency level of words he can spell correctly. We can also specify what spelling conventions he has mastered and can generalize. Examples of these analyses will be given in a later section. Finally on this first day of testing we may give a standardized test of reading. Our object here is not to establish a reading level but to observe the child's behavior in this kind of school task.

By the end of the first day of testing the diagnostician knows vastly more than the child's I.Q. and his reading and writing levels according to grade. He knows much about the quality of the child's language knowledge, his strengths, weaknesses, interests and apprehensions, his disposition to learn and his mechanisms for avoiding discomfort. One may observe, too, a variety of "soft" signs that may suggest the dyslectic condition. The child who pushes the erasure crumbs with his fingers rather than flicking them away with a flip of the wrist is noted. The ability to rotate the wrists rapidly is a time-honored neurological screening task. One notes the child's handwriting and drawing to see whether or not loops are smooth and round and the intersects clean and consistent. These are similar to the soft signs evaluated in the more formal Bender Measure of Visual Motor—Gestalt. One listens to the child's language and manner of defining and selecting words, for this may signal an hypothesis of mild speech pathology. The psychometrician will have made similar tentative judgments about the quality of performance and configuration of scores on the subtests of the Wechsler test. These independent judgments are combined and may strengthen or weaken one's beginning ideas about the child.

Finally, the case history of the child taken in the parent interview reveals the conditions of birth, development, health and school experience. The examiner learns much too about the parents—how well informed and understanding they are about their child, their attitudes and general life-style. These data also are shared, and together serve the diagnostician as he decides what further screening will be appropriate on the following day.

☐ Testing on Day Two

When adjustment problems appear to be present, the examiner will select an appropriate instrument to probe this area further. Similarly, screening may be done for vision, hearing, laterality, neurological integrity, for auditory and visual perception, and for memory span. All such tests are deemed optional, and the standard rule of "the least testing is the best" is strictly followed. Finally on the second day we usually try out informally some of the teaching activities that our sense of the child suggests may be appropriate.

☐ Parent Interviews and Reporting

The second parent interview is completed by about two o'clock on the second day so that relevant findings from this source may be followed up with the child as needed. These interviews serve a further and very important objective. They educate the parents and prepare them to think constructively about their role in directing their child's affairs. Throughout the first day our focus is upon this one child; when did he walk, when did he talk, what were his childhood ailments, accidents, and operations? What happened in kindergarten, in grade one, grade two? Only at the end do we discuss the "other children" and, as it were, recompose the family. In this setting the child emerges from "the other children" in great particularity. On day two we touch those points on which every parent and every child must reach an accommodation—the family meal, going to bed, temper control, allowance, chores, the neighborhood. It is thus that the social climate is constructed.

Our diagnostic work would go for naught if, at the last, we were not able to convey to the parents our sense of the child's care in terms of their world and in language they can understand and act upon. As clinicians we are neutral with regard to any particular life-style or manner of child management—authoritarian or permissive, volatile and expansive, restrained and inferential, rich or poor, it does not matter. What does matter, however, is that there be a climate of sufficient cohesion and consistency that child and parents can live in it with reasonable stability. In the course of these interviews parents very often think through these structural relationships and decide for themselves what changes or adjustments will prove most helpful for their children. Thus these sessions are not simply a source of data but in addition they are the springboard for corrective action.

Our final reports are presented orally to both parents, usually about one week after testing. In these sessions we present the capacity data in functional terms and give a full and direct accounting of what their child can do as a reader and writer. After this, we sketch in those factors that relate to the child's state of achievement or that may influence our expectations of further progress. Finally, in this context, we offer specific recommendations for home, school, and for special instruction if that is needed. When a written report is required it is prepared only after this final session with the parents.

☐ The Parents' Role

For parents, an understanding of the etiology of their child's case is of primary importance as it may help them reach constructive decisions in his behalf. Thus, if adjustment difficulties have rendered the child unfit to cope with learning tasks, they must understand that changes on this dimension must parallel correction of the reading problem itself, and they must work through some reasonable course of action to see that progress of this kind is made.

When the causes of the reading disability are or appear to be both central and aggravated, our prognosis is always guarded, for I am convinced that peripheral manipulation can *not* regroove or repair brain structure. For young children one may hope that some more adequate level of function may accrue over time and that learning will gradually occur if sound and supportive instruction is maintained. It is also possible to reason that such instruction may, by degrees, realize success as the learner is able to compensate for those discriminations that he is unable presently to make. Finally, one may hope that the apparent degree of dysfunction may stem in part from emotional overlay—fear, failure, frustration. Thus, again sustained supportive instruction may realize improvement.

In true cases of alexia and dyslexia, however, it is always possible that little or no progress in learning to read and write will be made. As a consequence, a central aspect of all remedial efforts must be to teach such individuals how to cope with the world as they are. My dyslexic friend provided me a good example of this point many years ago. It happened that he owned and knew how to fly a plane, and it also happened that he wished to visit a young lady on an offshore island in the southern United States. Unfortunately, he couldn't read a map or orient a map to a compass, nor could my most valiant efforts to teach him how to do so make it otherwise. As you would guess, he made the trip anyway. He followed the rail line to Cape Henry, flew to the smoke that was Norfolk, thence followed the crescent beach until he spotted the familiar lighthouse of Ocracoke. Nothing, he assured me, could be simpler. For the disabled reader, as with all the rest of us, love must find a way despite limitations and dangers. A good sense of humor and a good deal of pluck is the best remedial prescription that I know of.

Common Syndromes of Primary Reading Disability

There are many different kinds of centers to which children with learning disabilities come, and at each, the distribution of clinical syndromes is likely to differ. In a speech and hearing center, for example, reading problems related to aphasia will be far more frequently met than will other kinds of cases. In neurological/medical centers, one will find a far higher incidence of alexic and dyslexic patients. My own experience has been largely confined to a university reading center where the child's failure to learn in ordinary schools is the precipitating cause of referral. The pattern of syndromes that I will describe thus reflects this population.

Smallest in number, though prominent in recall, are those in the alexic/dyslexic category. These tend to subdivide into five general

types which I will label as follows: mixed symbols, patterning, meaning, modality, and brain-damaged.

☐ Mixed Symbols

My first subdivision, "mixed symbols," is the disability most popularly
recognized as dyslexia. Its outstanding clinical features are the persistence of primitive errors in letter production and recognition—reversals of *b* for *d* and *was* for *saw*, and the like. In addition, one notes
random errors of letter substitution and omission and inconsistency of
slant and form in handwriting. This is often accompanied by an ob-
durate failure to acquire a stable sight vocabulary. The classic features
of Gerstmann's syndrome, finger agnosia, dyscalcula, directional confusion are also frequently present. My friend of the airplane adventure
falls pretty clearly in this syndrome, as does the case described by
Geschwind in which writing and spelling alone were affected while
reading was achieved at a superior level. In both of these examples a
very high level of intelligence was manifest, though it would appear
that such a difficulty is not limited to the gifted.

One problem for the diagnostician in identifying this syndrome of
disability is the fact that some primitive errors—particularly reversals—are characteristic of all developing learners. In addition, very
similar gross error patterns may derive from chaotic learning experiences rather than from central disabilities. When these clinical features are accompanied by fair evidence that bad instruction has
occurred, I am inclined to view the case with somewhat greater
optimism and to reserve the label dyslexia until I can see what effect
sound instruction can produce.

In general I suppose that this syndrome is roughly the same as that
which Orton (1937) labeled strephosymbolia many years ago. His
theory then was that letter and word confusion were derived from a
failure in established language dominance, with the effect that symbols would arise willy-nilly in mirror form from the left or right hemisphere of the brain. Neurological research can no longer support this
appealing idea. I am inclined to believe instead that the seat of the
reading difficulty lies in the dominant hemisphere and specifically
with those mechanisms that must respond to the featural characteristics of written language.

Orton's theory led directly to a remedial technique that combines
stimulus reduction with direct synthetic instruction in letter formation
and letter-sound associations. This approach today is widely practiced, and the society bearing Orton's name has for many years provided energetic leadership in the study of dyslexia.

My principal qualm about what is now called the Orton-Gil-
lingham method is that I think it narrow in focus and therefore inappropriate for other kinds of dyslexia and reading disability in general.
I am also uncomfortable with any synthetic approach. Nonetheless, I

feel sure that letters must be learned if reading knowledge is to advance, and so, perhaps, there is some logic to a frontal attack upon the difficulty. My own persuasion, however, is to come at the problem obliquely. I have no confidence that nonfunctioning discriminations can be repaired by practice, and I think, therefore, the odds may be better if one provides a richer context and more support in an effort to bypass what may be wanting.

Thus, while I cannot really fault an initial, isolated concentration on letter study, my intuition is against it. Doubtless, however, when such teaching is handled with confidence and sensitivity and when the pupils are brought to natural language settings as early as possible, good results should, and in many cases have, attended the effort. A case in point might be the well-known "Ball, Stick, Bird Method," to which is joined supported reading in "action-packed" stories (Fuller 1974).

☐ Patterning Problems

The second dyslexic/alexic syndrome is quite different from the first. Popularly, it is much less widely recognized, yet in my experience, it is relatively common and often far more devastating to the learner. The critical inability in this syndrome appears to lie in activities requiring serial or patterned responses. The impact on the learner of reading appears to be a breakdown in his attempt to maintain a temporal-spatial match or coordination. Intuitively one can see this would impair his opportunity of forming a stable concept of wordness. Moreover, should this in some measure be accomplished, further internal analysis of words would be considerably hampered. Some case examples here may help illustrate the condition.

Richard was a bright lad of fourteen who, however, could only identify his name and a few other words. On the other hand, he knew all of his letters and could tell you the sound or sounds that each might represent. He had been read to abundantly and had a wealth of knowledge. He had imagination, humor, and charm. He could not learn his multiplication tables, but he could tell you when, in a given problem, one should multiply. He understood the concept of prime numbers but could not point to the primes in a serial list of numbers. When we succeeded in placing him in a modern junior high school, we found he could not find his way from room to room but had to resort to cruising systematically until he spotted a familiar face.

Richard was with us for two academic years, during which time we worked with him directly on reading for an hour in the early morning and then helped him with homework in the afternoon. He easily learned the tracing technique (Fernald 1943) and succeeded in amassing a sight vocabulary of perhaps 100 to 200 words. He could reread dictated accounts with our help, but not without it. His word knowledge did not and has not advanced much beyond that point.

Presently Richard is completing his senior year at college, where he has achieved fine grades in demanding subjects. He has done so by making use of taped books and a paid reading aide. He drives his own car and navigates in his own way, but he does not read. His subjective report of his experience with words is that when he looks at a word it falls away before he can see it. But note that this does not happen with individual letters or most other things that he attends to.

A second example of a similar deficit is that of a young woman in her twenties who was injured in a motorcycle accident. Though she had previously been a good student, she now experienced much difficulty with spelling and found reading unusually troublesome. In testing her I found she could read easily all that she knew on a relatively automatic basis before the injury, but when confronted with an unfamiliar word or phrase, "Sargasso Sea," for example, she became extremely tense and almost helpless, saying, "I can't, I can't." If I told her the word, she could then advance, calling it correctly at successive meetings in the passage. In spelling, the pattern was the same. Automatic words were no problem, but those that had to be constructed part-by-part serially threw her into confusion. One can readily imagine the discomfort she experienced attempting to pursue a course in art history!

We were able to help this client devise a support system for reading (in this case her helpful student husband) and as her understanding of the problem improved and her confidence recovered, she found herself able to exert sufficient analysis to proceed quite well on her own. Spelling remained marginal, but improvement here too was accomplished. I conclude that prior knowledge, plus a lowering of tension, here served to alleviate the effect of the deficit. In Richard's case, however, the needed store of knowledge simply could not be gained.

I have described these cases in some detail not only because I feel they are not widely recognized as a syndrome but also because they illustrate dramatically that the teaching of letter and letter-sound relationships is not the be-all and end-all of reading instruction, remedial or otherwise. Both of these subjects had a full command of letters and the sounds they represented, but the one never learned and the other nearly floundered for want of an altogether different coordinate facility. These cases illustrate too our inability to do more than try to understand and try to help. We cannot get inside and change things. If help does not suffice, the person so affected must learn to cope in other ways.

☐ Meaning Dysfunction

The third syndrome that I would like to suggest in this category is altogether different from the preceding two in that it has nothing at all to do with letter recognition, word knowledge, or well-phrased oral reading, but with meaning. What appears to be misfunctioning is that mechanism, whatever it may be, that conveys minimal graphic features to long-term storage or "gist."

Consider the case of William. At ten years of age he could score well on a Wechsler test, about 115, converse intelligently about his school subjects, run, play, and do athletic things. He was a hobbyist, a beginning craftsman, and he could read aloud in a fifth-grade level reader fluently and with good expression. William could not, however, answer comprehension questions about what he read, or give you the gist of what he read, either silently or aloud, if the passage exceeded a length that would hold in short-term memory. Testwise this placed him at about a first-grade reading comprehension level.

William's difficulty should be distinguished from those in which want of intellectual strategy is the problem or from those in which meaning is "blocked" by neurosis. His condition is superficially similar to the hyperlexic described by Mehegan and Dreifuss (1972), although in hyperlexics, oral expression is wanting, and no meaning transpires at all. William's case also differs from those in which a mild expressive aphasia may interfere with word perception. In twenty years I have met but two other children who fit this syndrome precisely.

I had the opportunity to work with William for nearly three years, during which time some progress was made, but there was no magic cure that I could find. My strategy was to work from those bits that he could hold and try to help him develop a strategy for building upon them. For example, he would read a sentence, tell me its gist (usually a very close paraphrase), then tell me what the next sentence would probably say. Then he would read, affirm, predict and so on. From this framework, we worked to larger "bites" and by degrees to more complex material. By age thirteen William was able to read fifth-grade level material with reasonable control. His achievement, however, was still out of keeping with his intellectual abilities and with the demands that an ordinary academic circumstance must require of him as a reader and student.

Examination of this syndrome makes one point clear: mixed symbols is not the only class of reading disability. Remedial reading instruction moving blindly in the dark can seek to help and may have some ameliorative effects, but often it can achieve but limited goals.

☐ Modality Deficit

The fourth dyslexic syndrome, which I distinguish, is possibly a bogus one, or at least it is one about which I have mixed feelings and some doubts. I will call it a modality deficit. It might as well, however, be termed a problem of short-term memory and/or an associative learning difficulty. None of these is truly satisfactory. On the basis of diagnostic screening, many children with severe retardation in reading will be found to score lower on auditory than on visual tests of memory span, and, not surprisingly, lowest of all on memory span tests involving random letters. I have never been able to make sense of such findings other than to suppose they must reflect some adjustment attentional factors. With the visual presentation, the subject has control of his own perusal and thus may fare better. Furthermore, the fundamental difference between visual perception of words and visual perception of objects (i.e., pictures) makes inference from one task to the other very difficult. Occasionally, I have found a dramatic difference between the visual and auditory modes. In most of these children, there was also evidence, by electroencephalography, of central nervous system dysfunction.

Finally, difficulty in making association within and across modalities is often held to be an underlying cause of reading difficulty. In my opinion, however, this is not so. Certainly it is characteristic of all children who are failing to learn to read, for whatever cause, that they "know" words one minute and forget them the next. I am inclined to believe, however, that it is the underlying knowledge that is deficient not the association that bonds the concept to a label.

Despite this array of uncertainty, I am nonetheless willing to entertain the possibility of the existence of a preferred modality which may stem from some functional or neurological cause. Since reading certainly does require the harmonizing of perceptual modes, doubtless such an unbalance could prove disruptive.

One of the most extreme cases in this syndrome was Peter, whose auditory tests for memory span fell some seven mental age years below those he attained for the visual tasks. There was no evidence of hearing loss, high frequency or otherwise. This youngster had experienced a protracted high fever as an infant and had lost some motor function throughout his right side. From this, of course, one infers damage to the left hemisphere of the brain.

Peter was a bright lad, a pretty good athlete, despite his mild disability, and plucky both physically and intellectually. At the time of testing he was nine years of age and able to read at a beginning second grade level. He was concerned about his failure and was having some trouble with both temper control and enuresis.

We placed Peter in a perfectly ordinary reading instructional program—abundant silent reading of all kinds, word-sort activities as appropriate, and all of the writing we could induce. The only modification we made was to flash tachistoscopically, rather than dictate, words he wanted to practice for spelling. At the end of the year Peter tested well above his grade level. Thereafter he moved to a different city where he entered and succeeded in an advanced placement classroom.

I do not offer Peter's case as a testimonial to our teaching. We often do our best with less salutory results. Peter's ease simply illustrates my lack of understanding of alexia that turns upon a modality deficit.

☐ Brain Damage

The final alexic syndrome I will advance is that associated with the well-documented condition of global brain damage. The characteristics of the condition have been carefully described by Sheldon R. Rappaport (1964). The hallmarks of this syndrome are hyperactivity, compulsivity, figure-ground perceptual confusion, and ego deficiency. In full flower it is a devastating condition requiring skilled clinical aid across the board and for a very long time.

In essence, once again metaphorically, it is as if a filter mechanism were wanting such that competing stimuli cannot be shielded out. Thus the booming, buzzing reality of the senses is a chaotic, distracting constant. Medication has in many cases succeeded in effecting a better level of focus, after which learning, including learning how to behave, becomes possible.

The best-known instructional strategy for brain-damaged children is that of Cruickshank and his associates (1961) in which stimulus distraction is reduced to the minimum. Work is carried on in a cubicle with bare walls and even light. Materials and tasks are applied only one at a time, and the instructor maintains a composed and even level of personal disposition. In general, this approach makes sense; it has, in my opinion, a place in the repertoire of the remedial teacher. I would counsel, however, that each step forward in such an instructional plan should be accompanied by a step outward into the world. Application of this technique to all pupils in a remedial center is not justified.

The one child of this general type with whom I worked longest was Joe. He was, when I first met him, totally illiterate and on the surface quite mad. He had suffered from encephalitis at age seven and eventually was placed in solitary confinement in an institution. He was retrieved from this sad condition by his brave mother who taught him to mind and to do what he could on his own. His spoken language had revived and flourished. His behavior was controlled, but bizarre. When other children came home from school his mother would bring him indoors, for they taunted him with the label, "Rubber Brain." As you will see, he understood them.

Joe's condition was not so dire as that of the child who is so afflicted from infancy. He had had seven years of normal development though he could not remember it. In addition, he had the strength of his parents to lean upon, and this was never withdrawn.

In one of my early sessions with Joe, he dictated a fantastic story about a blackbird who was hated by all the others because he was stupid. At last this bird flew away to a volcano crying, "Kill me volcano, kill me!" But it chanced that this was a Magic Volcano and instead of killing him, it turned him into a super bird with super powers. The tale advanced in some shocking ways, and the theme was often returned to, but at the end Blacky flew to Joe's window and they talked. Thus I knew that though he had suffered deeply, Joe also knew who he was. He was angry and hurt, but not mad.

For a long time I worked with Joe in quite private conditions. He required absolute order and would be terribly upset if his pencil, for example, were not in the exact position he had left it the day before. During this period, he learned some words by tracing, and he dictated a great deal. His ability to sustain attention grew almost imperceptibly at first, but gains were being made, and I knew that this was so. At the end of two years, he began to learn to read. At the end of four, I was able to place him in a regular junior high school where he began the tough job of learning to cope. It was a tremendous step back into the world. All that fall our language sessions were spent simply in my listening as he talked these problems through.

By spring we were again working in the big room with others and making progress too. Then one day he turned to me with a sort of mischievous smile and said, apropos of nothing really, "You know, I don't need magic anymore." And, of course, I knew then that he did not.

Though now it is many years later, the pain is still fresh when I write that Joe died the next summer. He, however, would scoff at my emotion, for he had been to the mountain and returned with amazing wisdom. His learning is for me a legacy to all those who need but a parent's and a teacher's trust and time to work things through. There is no case I will not tackle on his behalf, for he showed me what the mind and heart can do that is quite beyond my own understanding.

So much for dyslexia. It is a real form of reading disability. Its diagnosis is relatively easy when clinical and medical indications are clear. Where the condition must be assumed wholly on behavioral indicators, however, it is far more difficult to be certain. In the last analysis it is the obdurateness of the dysfunction that marks this particular condition.

Regardless of the surface signs, for nearly all seriously retarded readers make errors similar to those of the dyslexic, when social and academic conditions loom as highly probable causes of failure, I am most inclined to avoid the label dyslexia. In the great majority of such cases, corrective counseling and very ordinary but carefully managed instruction yields, in good time, very normal learning progress.

☐ Incidence of Dyslexia/Alexia

In my experience, dyslexia accounts for a very small proportion of the cases of reading failure that presently concern us. My estimate is, of course, based on my definition of the term and upon my observation of school conditions as well as the diagnostic tally in the two university centers in which I have served. From this perspective, I find every reason to agree with that figure declared by Emmett Betts (1946) of two to five percent of the population. One would expect such a figure to remain fairly constant, and I believe indeed that it has.

Reading failure, however, does not remain constant across social-cultural groups, schools and school districts and not even, I think, over time. In the ghettos and among certain of the rural poor the incidence may be as high as fifty or even sixty percent. Among juvenile delinquents the figure most often reported is eighty percent. No skewed curve of intelligence or wild outbreak of abnormality could account for these learning failures. I believe, therefore, that we have most valid grounds to argue that the major incidence of reading failure stems from correctible (though not always easily correctible) causes. I think it follows, moreover, that any serious corrective effort must focus on correcting our communities as well as our institutions of education.

Common Syndromes of Secondary Reading Disability

Just as dyslexia is found to occur in some general syndromes, so do cases of reading failure fall into discernable groups or patterns. I tend to divide such cases along the following lines: written language deprivation, developmental lag, deficiencies of will and self-reliance, and pedagogical insult.

☐ Written Language Deprivation

The discussion of reading readiness in chapter 5 has already provided a detailed account of those language experiences that I believe to be necessary for beginning to learn to read. Thus I need merely repeat that an absence of such experience is most likely to result in failure. This is particularly true if children so deprived are set to a learning schedule that advances on a surface conditioning basis. Lacking a tacit comprehension of letter and word, of the cadence and form of written language, and perhaps most of all its purpose and role in their lives, children cannot be expected to respond well to any standard beginning reading material, nor do I think that some novel method should be sought out to teach them by. Today, the DISTAR program is widely touted as "the approach" that will succeed with "those children." Methodological comparison studies support its effectiveness. I doubt it. Teaching method, moreover, is not the important issue here, instead we should address ourselves to the correction of those environmental conditions that perpetrate these reading deficiencies.

It will be recalled that the Maori children described by Marie Clay (1976) did make progress but that progress came late—that is, in grades two and three. That this happened in those New Zealand classrooms is evidence that the teachers there maintained a wholesome and active language environment until those children learned enough to make a natural beginning. No special education or other heroic efforts were necessary, nor can one compress the time it takes to learn those necessary things. We can and should do likewise in our schools.

To accomplish this end we will first have to become more discriminating in our judgments about what children know when they enter school. I tried in the section on readiness to sketch in those procedures that would make such an evaluation possible. It is also easy enough to devise a simple informal screening instrument that will give a fairly accurate evaluation of this knowledge. Second, we will have to revise our concept of failure itself. If a child does learn enough in two years so that he begins to read in grade three, then this must be recognized as success. We must undertake to be accountable for productivity and progress on the part of pupils rather than for their meeting some arbitrary normative levels of achievement.

On the community front, I would like to see more efforts of the kind so well executed by "Reading is Fundamental." There should be more story hours in libraries and churches. High school boys and girls could render yeoman service by reading to young children who lack this advantage. And on television let there be some stories read, in place of those manic and bizarre oral language cartoons. If we truly care about literacy, steps of this sort should be taken. Presently it is, I think, our largest area of social failure.

☐ Developmental Lag

This label is not a pretty one, but I am sick and tired of euphemisms like "the exceptional child"; so I will stick with developmental lag. It denotes a level of ignorance and unskillfulness that derives from later-than-average physical/cognitive maturation. It is relatively independent of both social advantage and intelligence, and the range of difference among children spans the normal range. This is a phenomenon that we recognize and accept with tact and good judgment in physical development. In this respect, I think of my son and his cousin who were born one week apart. The one became six feet tall at age twelve, the other the same at fifteen. They did, of course, look a bit like Mutt and Jeff as they trotted around together during those years, but at least no one required that they wear the same size shoe. In school, however, this often is not so.

The quick sprouter cognitively often has some problems, but for the most part precocity does not alarm us. Indeed, typically, we reward it too much. The other end of the spectrum, however, the late-developing child, the laggard, alarms and annoys us very much. We press him to the norm, and when we and he both fail, we pass the buck. The educational boat pulls out, and he never again can board it. From time to time such children are allowed to repeat a grade, but this often does little good, for they simply fail to do again what they failed to do before for want of more basic understandings.

The pedagogical answer to this problem is necessarily similar to that which must apply to those who have experienced language deprivation. Teachers must be better apprised of the language competencies of their pupils. They must teach in a manner that paces to this knowledge rather than to surface responses. It is useful to recognize that chimpanzees may, with tremendous effort on the part of a skilled trainer, be taught to tap out a few communications on a computer. Similar efforts may yield similar meager results with children if we disregard their human mentality as we teach. Such is the unfortunate condition of a good number of reading failures.

I recall quite well one little girl who had this experience in a popular programmed reading series. In grade one she filled in the blanks of books one through six. Failing the competency test in grade two, she was restarted in book three and filled in the blanks through book eight. Failing the competency test in grade three, she was started again in book three and filled in the blanks—the same blanks—through book nine.

There really was nothing wrong with this child except that at grade one she could make no sense of what she did, and by grade three the materials were so shopworn that no sense was made of them either. Her teachers, with the best intentions in the world, did allow her to repeat—in this sense the boat had not pulled out—but their evaluative eyes remained fixed on the responses instead of on the child. So long as the blanks were filled, the appearance of progress was there. It is this that is so devilish about such materials.

☐ Deficiencies of Will and Self-Reliance

A more intractable and deeper-seated cause of reading failure stems from a deficiency of will and self-reliance, which condition itself must be thought to have roots in the personality and the developmental experiences of the learner. The harsh conditions of poverty and neglect contribute to this state as freely as do those of overprotection and spoiling. While we often hear most about those children whose despair results in antisocial behavior, I am inclined to believe that far more children express this discomfort through inaction and withdrawal. The most palpable characteristic of those classrooms I have visited where conditions of this kind prevailed is a want of daring and a level of aspiration that could take no measured chances with error. True learning depends on a risk-taking readiness of mind.

I have observed very similar conditions in the segregated classrooms that were maintained for so long in the border states and in the South. It was as if those black teachers, intuitively and wisely knowing the danger to their children of intellectual assertion, taught them systematically to mind, to conform, to be right or be silent. The seeds of repression and riot are sown in such settings as those, and I am profoundly grateful that our courts and our legislators have had the wisdom to decree a change.

It seems to me of the greatest national importance that we face this aspect of intellectual growth squarely. The ability to read is indivisible from it. We must achieve better-balanced and more salubrious communities, and our classrooms must offer both the challenge and the protection that risk requires. This does not mean that we must flood our schools with plastic toys and bric-a-brac. The child playing on the kitchen floor with pots and pans is as advantaged as one who messes about with the latest educational toy (provided that on the floor there are no stray knives, exposed electrical outlets, and things to hurt and maim).

Overprotection is a relatively well-recognized disrupter of learning, though it often occurs in variations that are surprising. I have sometimes urged my undergraduate students to observe the mother and child scene in a local supermarket in order to learn about the kinds of controls young children experience and learn to manipulate. No one pattern is perfect or correct in an absolute sense. Both formal control and measured permissiveness work equally well, provided the management system is reasonably consistent. It is when the child has no ground rules to work against that he gives up or runs amok.

Children must work through their destiny and take responsibility for their own actions by degrees and as they are able. The well-intentioned parent who sets his child to his homework task each night will soon find that the child will relegate all such planning to the parent. It is a simple matter of economy. Why should he plan when to study? That job has already been done.

In our parent interviews we comb as carefully as we can through the growing up and developmental data in order to reconstruct the management style and the child's responses to it. We ask at one point, for example, when Tommy could wash and dress for himself. Here we are not so interested in hygiene as we are in when this responsibility was turned over to the child. Since there is almost no child that I know of who did not want to stay up a little later than his parents wished, we ask them to describe the going-to-bed scene. We are interested to learn who won and how! These interviews are truly fascinating, and they do bear importantly upon learning. Here is an amusing example.

One fine young farming couple was blessed with a bright little boy who soon became "the little man." He followed Daddy about and adopted his style quite thoroughly. Mother kept house; Father and Billy did the farming. When I inquired about Billy's likes and dislikes in food, Mother reported that he couldn't abide having butter put on his toast when it was served; indeed, just the other morning he had said, "You *know* I don't like butter on my toast!"

"Ah, and how did you handle that?"

"Well, I really hadn't been thinking. I got him a dry piece."

Now can you imagine this "little man" arriving in a first-grade classroom directed by a wise, older teacher who had very clear ideas about what children should and should not do? It was simply disastrous. It took Billy all year long to find out who he was and wasn't and during the course of this very important bit of education there was little time left for learning to read. The next year he did learn very nicely, and so, I think, did Mother and Father.

Some forms of overprotection are unfortunately very difficult to avoid. This is particularly true for the chronically ill child where stress must be avoided, as with the asthmatic youngster, for example. Their experiences with stress and how to deal with it are simply underexercised, and this places them at a disadvantage when they do not know and must learn. For such children, allowances must be made and support provided. It has been my experience that they tend to do better when, at a little older age, they can begin to understand the nature of their problem.

Another curious disrupter of learning that fits this general syndrome is that which stems from a want of intellectual experience and valuing. It is as if the world were perceived as composed wholly of extrinsic rewards, while the inner satisfactions of knowing are disregarded.

I recall one client who arrived at the center in a very large Cadillac with his high school age daughter. He brought an expensive tape recorder to our interview, during which the price of nearly everything in their lives, of which there was much, was duly reported. Father was a self-made man and as sincere and honest in his way as he could be. He had tackled the world of things, and he had won—things. Olivia, the daughter, was bright—she read perfectly fluently—she worked hours and hours on her lessons, yet she flunked again and again. Where understanding is not the goal, the plan, and the reward, study tasks soon disintegrate and defeat the student however hard he tries.

To restructure the motivational base of a learner is, in my experience, the most difficult of all corrective efforts. It is for this reason that I am so much concerned about the emphasis placed in our schools on norms, grades, token rewards, and the like, at the expense of that larger experience of the quest for knowledge for its own sake. Mechanized materials of instruction—surface questions and surface answers—have this same debilitating effect. That is why I am committed to our need for real books by real authors in our language curriculum. But this does not mean that students do not also have to learn how to master a subject thoroughly and in detail when circumstances require such attainment.

Consider Mr. Cartwright, for example. He was a second-year medical student, a Princeton graduate, with very high verbal exam scores. He seemed, however, quite unable to pass the physiology exam, and both he and his advisor had concluded that he must be suffering from dyslexia. It took but a little time to discern that he had read his physiology text to *understand* it only. Thereafter, he had worked through mock exams in which information to be reported was randomly scattered. The more he tried to study these, the more confused, rattled, and forgetful he became. Obviously he wasn't dyslexic; he just didn't know how to study physiology. One of my students showed him how he must reread his text using understanding and self-discipline to achieve a comprehensive recall. Only a session or two was needed.

That spring he passed the exam with flying colors, and a year later, after graduation, he made a special trip to my office to thank us for "saving his academic life." I was glad indeed to have been able to do so simple a thing. Yet it does seem to me that such understandings could and should be conveyed in the high school years. Also, I am distressed that the specter, "dyslexia," should haunt so many to whom it simply does not apply.

☐ Educational Insult

As a category of reading failure, educational insult is also an ugly term. Yet it is one that I think we should accept and do something about. There are simply thousands upon thousands of children whose learning difficulties are compounded and aggravated by inappropriate teaching. This need not and should not be the case. It is my belief that this condition arises not because teachers are unable or unwilling to do better but because they are uninformed about reading as a process and in many cases not allowed to rely on their common sense and judgment.

Unfortunately, our undergraduate and graduate education courses in reading today are grossly inadequate. This is true not so much in the course hours allotted to this study but in the content of the courses that are offered. In all too many cases, these courses consist simply of "learning" to read a set of teacher's manuals and of "studying" how to tend the teaching machine. How we came into such a predicament is fairly clear historically; what is necessary now is that we change it, and it will require a sober and long-range effort by all of us. Teachers must learn to pace instruction and provide exercise for the language knowledge that each pupil possesses at the time. This is not an idealized responsibility but an absolutely necessary one. We must discard programmed materials of instruction and replace them with materials that have integrity and flexibility. We must abandon the abstract concept of the norm—that hypothetical average child—and teach each child as we find him.

Many kinds of reading failure derive from conditions that educators cannot control directly—cultural deprivation, physiological development, and social-emotional difficulties. The teacher and the system at large, however, must respond to these circumstances as they exist. Failure to do so can result only in a further disruption of learning and a compounding of the learner's problems. It is this that I construe to be educational insult.

Consider the child who begins to show every kind of tension sign as August wanes and September looms ahead. Consider the one who is nauseous every morning at the prospect of going to school. Look at the knuckles of a twelve-year-old pressed white against a pencil as he tries to write. Listen to the stammering ritual efforts of the defeated learner trying to read aloud. Study the errors of the crippled speller— wild errors, reversals, omissions, insertions that make no sense. Look into the face of a bright child who has concluded from the evidence of failure that he is stupid. Reflect upon the adjustment devices these children must gradually adopt to protect themselves from this pain.

This is the price we pay each year for our want of understanding. So long as we insist that all children must learn to read at one time and so long as we apply closed programs of instruction and blind systems of evaluation, we will continue to reap this harvest. I do not here mean that educators should be soft, passive, permissive, or juvenile. To the contrary, they must be adult, demanding, active, and rigorous. But the tasks that are applied must be those that children can with best effort do and in so doing learn from them. And these tasks must further be conducted in a context that makes sense; a curriculum must exist that is more than a ritual of skills.

Rather than belabor this point further, I want now to present some word-recognition and spelling data from a selection of children who were failing to learn to read. To these I will try to apply what our studies of word knowledge suggest that each child knows about words and what he might profitably learn next.

Diagnosis of Word Knowledge

First let us look at the spelling productions of two seven-year-olds who came to the McGuffey Reading Center for diagnosis. Karen appears more advanced in word knowledge than Mike—twenty words correctly spelled against two. Yet as one looks more closely at these children, one notes some similarities (Chart 1).

In the second-level list, Karen evidences a remarkably consistent letter-name strategy as she invents spellings for those words she has not yet learned on a sight basis. Observe the omitted preconsonantal nasal in THIG for *think*, the vocalic r spelling of FRM for *farm*, and the SORE for *story* (never mind for now the omitted t.) If you will accept as a kinetic reversal the r and t in WERT, rendering it WETR, then you will see the common letter-name substitution of e for short i, the omission of n, then t plus vocalic r for *ter* which is exactly as it should be for *winter*. Note also the e for short i substitution in DED for *did*. One could go on in this way—not accounting for everything, of course, but making, nonetheless, a strong case that this child's concept of word is at a late letter-name stage. She has also obviously been attentive and learned a fair number of words in their correct form. This commendable effort, however, was not sufficient to achieve a power score typical of an achieving second grader.

Now let's consider Mike. His spellings on the first-grade list are

Chart 1. Spelling Performance by Two Seven-Year-Old Children on
an Inventory of High Frequency Words

Karen				Mike	
Level I		Level II		Level I	
and		thig	(think)	cam	(come)
me		frm	(farm)	hee	(he)
some		pit	(pet)	maru	(mother)
little		sore	(story)	aed	(and)
had		wert	(winter)	was	
you'r	(your)	and		aeh	(have)
are		one		bow	(do)
mie	(my)	shon	(show)	at	(it)
bee	(be)	wret	(were)	her	(here)
she		get		can	
the		evy	(every)	mae	(may)
up		Ded	(did)		
				Nonsense words	
am		geen	(green)		
hose	(horse)	mining	(morning)	lat	(lat)
no		ovr	(over)	saet	(sait)
all		sad		rat	(ret)
one		am		let	(leat)
an		to	(two)		
yes		Aeg	(eggs)		

markedly deviant; that is, they do not evidence the substitution patterns typical of a normal developmental strategy. He is consistent but
deviant in using *a* for [u] in *come* and *mother*, which in "letter name"
would actually be spelled COM, MOTHR. Moreover, the *r* and *u* are
totally variant. The *a* in AT is deviant because the word *it* in letter
name would be spelled ET. One sees a kinetic reversal of the *h* in *have*
and a static reversal of the *b* for *d* in *do*. While *ae* in *and* represents
short *a*, the expected would be *a* alone. Thus, *and* should be spelled
AD (he did omit the preconsonantal nasal *n*), while *have* would be
spelled HAV.

But now look at Mike's spelling pattern when applied to nonsense
words. It is nearly perfect letter-name invention. What then may we
conclude from this? My hunch is that this lad has *not* been very attentive to words and has not learned them. In his efforts to produce those
words he *ought* to know, he now is disregarding what in fact he tacitly
knows and is floundering around by hook and by crook to produce
something that will do.

Both of these children appear to me to be quite normal in their
developing word knowledge and nearly equally advanced. Both need
those word-study activities that lead from the beginning reading to the

early reading transition. In Karen's case, the likelihood of progress is quite good, provided that reasonable support is maintained while this needed knowledge is assimilated. Mike, on the other hand, has already begun to turn away from what he knows and to adapt a primitive guessing strategy. One will need to settle this youngster down and take the learning pressure off until he can "get out of the sandbox" and begin attending to tasks. Forced word learning and forced phonics for this lad at this point would soon turn him into a first-class pseudo-dyslexic.

Next let's look at three nine-year-olds, Sam, Bruce, and Chuck (Chart 2). All are reading failures; none is dyslexic, and they differ interestingly in their state-of-word knowledge. Sam is at a transitional stage, that is, he is correct and largely consistent with short vowel patterns and tends to employ markers, though not always correctly, with long vowels. Thus, MENNY, for *many*, REDDY for *ready*, LADHING for *laughing*, MISIS for *Mrs.*, and CRIY for *cry*. Some letter-name spellings, however, are present—MOST for *must*, TECH for *teach*. He is ambivalent about consonant doubling with inflectional endings and appears in general to be settling into a fairly rigid letter-sound matching approach, while disregarding the miscellaneous possibilities. One might think him fairly diligent in learning what he is taught but lacking in venture. This is a condition well suited to producing a chronically bad speller.

Bruce's misspellings are at a lower level of development than Sam's. The letter-name invention is seen in the following constructions; *E* for *i* in WEH for *with*, unmarked *i* in LIC for *like*, *a* for *a* in HAW for *have*, and the unmarked *i* in FI for *five*. It appears, however, that he has learned, and indeed learned far too well, "the short sound for u." See JUM for *come*, MU for *mother*, WUS for *was*, UN for *on*, UF for *of*, MUT for *must*, MUG for *much*. The same kind of learning doubtless accounts for the first e of MENE for *many*, while the final E is a typical letter-name construction.

My judgment here is that Bruce has just about fixated at an early letter-name level. He has tried at the surface level to apply a letter-sound, phonic-matching strategy on top of this. It has not worked, and he is giving up. He simply fails to complete *mother* and *five*, and he composes a crude configurative match, WRTRE for *water*.

Chuck is in deep trouble indeed. He is fixated at, or has reverted to, a prephonetic or pre-letter-name state. Beyond the correctly rendered initial consonant, his vowel substitutions and endings are deviant, random, and stereotyped but roughly sufficient to achieve a nonlegal word figure. It happens that this lad had suffered from a chronic physical handicap and some quite aggravated adjustment problems related thereto. This is a case where the will to cope is largely wanting. Parent-child counseling will be a necessary first step before a new beginning can be made toward reawakening the quest for word knowledge.

When not only the power of a child's word knowledge but also the

Chart 2. Spelling Performance of Three Nine-Year-Old Children on
an Informal Spelling Inventory

Sam			Bruce		
Level II		Level III	Level I		Level II

Level II		Level III		Level I		Level II	
table	(table)	news		Jum	(come)	table	
you		things		to		you	
bed		six		he		bed	
most	(must)	tech	(teach)	me	(mother)	mut	(must)
had		roof		and		had	
water		farmer		wus	(was)	wrtre	(water)
menny	(many)	walked		in		mene	(many)
five		reddy	(ready)	do		fi	(five)
other		part		it		uthr	(other)
much		carry		can		mug	(much)
house		place		weh	(with)		
pull		laphing	(laughing)	un	(on)		
saw		wall		lic	(like)		
criy	(cry)	laphed	(laughed)	see			
		holding		i			
		wached	(watched)	haw	(have)		
		misis	(Mrs.)	we			
		Irly	(early)	her	(here)		
		walking		uf	(of)		
		siting	(sitting)				
		clean					
		gray stores					
		cream light					

Chuck			
Level I		Level II	
cuom	(come)	haim	(hand)
go		boum	(down)
you		con	(cow)
he		puint	(party)
muom	(mother)	sull	(shall)
a	(and)	hain	(had)
want	(was)		
in		*Nonsense Words*	
do		luae	(luz)
can		aitt	(op)
wian	(with)	saay	(suf)
on		daay	(dop)

Chart 2. (*cont.*)

Chuck			
Level I		Level II	
like		jayy	(jex)
see		niaay	(nade)
I		kaoy	(fip)
hain	(have)	Bayn	(baz)
we		klll	(kak)
here		goom	(gope)
of		blly	(bock)
		Baacn	(pij)
		Zlla	(zilp)
		jllo	(chupe)
		Saom	(stum)

qualitative level of that knowledge can be assessed, one is in a far better position to make recommendations about what kinds of word-study tasks will be appropriate. In addition, through knowing what kinds of errors constitute normal developmental learning, one can then identify errors that are deviant. Studying these in relation to a child's age, intelligence, and educational experience can then very often suggest the nature, cause, and character of the deviation, and so, by extension, what might best be done to help.

In years past the only prescriptions available to the crippled speller/reader were to (1) memorize words in serial letter order and/or visually by flash cards, (2) study phonics, and (3) study spelling rules. Of these, 1 and 2 are still the core antidote of most corrective teaching efforts today.

One good outcome of reading diagnosis in the 1940s was the identification of what were called "instructional levels" based on the subject's power in identification and production of words. Thus a score of 100 at Level I, 75 at Level II, and 50 at Level III would indicate that spelling should be taught, or reteaching should begin, at the second-grade level. This had the effect of removing the retarded reader/speller from a hopelessly frustrating task. Beyond this point, however, the prescription remained the same—memorization plus phonics.

An insight about the child's qualitative knowledge of word provides a long-needed change of view. To begin with, we know that the memorization of words "at sight" and by letter sequence must and does take place. We also know that this avenue is limited by the underlying state of orthographic knowledge a child has attained. Thus it is not possible to correct a deficiency in spelling by memorization alone. Second, we know that phonics instruction, as traditionally conceived, is almost totally ill founded. Children do not need to be taught the phonemic elements of words; they can deal with these perfectly. What they do need to learn progressively are those conventions for abstraction by which their spelling system is removed from a strict phonetic rendering. In short, the primitive character of children's first spelling derives from the fact that they spell phonetically on the basis of letter names. To the degree that we teach children more phonics, that is, one-to-one letter-sound associations, the more primitive their spelling becomes. We saw this clearly in the spelling errors of Bruce where short *u* was rendered consistently *u* in error after error, among the most high frequency words, *of*, *on*, *mother*, for example. One sees this often in the spelling cripple's rendering of *was*, as WUZ, which the developmental speller will render initially as WOS and, early on, correctly as *WAS*.

What the child must do in order to learn to spell is to compare his own natural and powerfully derived "ideas" about how a word is spelled with the way it actually is spelled in his particular writing system. This condition requires both that he see, learn, and remember how words in fact are spelled and that he continue to exercise and by degrees modify his tacit guess. The evidence necessary for a final, finished, and flawless inner sense of spelling will require many years, near full maturity, and ample practice. Sheer memory, including the facility to attend and direct the focus of memory, is necessary but alone is not sufficient for this progress. Equally important is the task of meeting, practicing, and internalizing those conventions by which English spelling is given order.

Thus, if we are to help those children who have faltered, it is necessary that we identify what they know about their orthographic system and also the degree to which they have ventured, for whatever reason, down false trails. If their difficulties stem from some physiological impairment that deflects analysis, memory, or both, our efforts toward correction must be sustained but realistic. If, on the other hand, they have merely misconceived the problem, then we must return to the basics and show them the way that leads forward.

Most examples I have used so far have involved younger children. My idea of returning to basics may be illustrated by an analysis of spelling errors produced by a fourteen-year-old. He was a bright lad who had done well in elementary school, but he read very little and quite slowly and wrote as little as possible. In the last two years he shot up to a height of six feet four inches, and his grades in school had suddenly dropped to a marginal pass. Quite obviously he had "gone to sleep" during those junior high school years.

Now notice the errors that he made on a spelling inventory and in writing a short essay (Chart 3). Clearly, he shows mastery of basic single-syllable word structure. What is wanting is some sense of the regularities that hold for polysyllabic words. On the second day of testing we experimented with his errors in order to see how responsive he might be to a word-study task.

When asked to spell *real*, *practical*, *personal*, *appear*, and *regard*, Tom rendered each correctly except for the last, which he spelled *REGUARD*. Next, when asked to spell the inflected forms, he wrote

Chart 3. Spelling Performance of a Fourteen-Year-Old Boy on an Informal Spelling Inventory and on a Sample Writing Task

VI		VII	
centural	(central)	practaly	(practically)
surving	(serving)	colected	(collected)
		banage	(bandage)
		behaveure	(behavior)
		personaly	(personally)
		madan	(madam)
		straiten	(straighten)

VIII		Writing	
apperaing	(appearing)	realy	(really)
regaurless	(regardless)	famly	(family)
equistance	(existence)	skared	(scared)
finansial	(financial)	wourms	(worms)
persuit	(pursue)	baite	(bait)
disappont	(disappoint)	cacch	(catch)
subscription	(subscription)		
kindergatren	(kindergarten)		
misionaly	(missionary)		
forewarded	(forwarded)		
evedence	(evidence)		

REALLY, PRACTICALY, PERSONALLY, APPEARING, and *REGUARD-LESS,* and when asked why he treated *practicaly* differently from the others, he added the missing *l*.

After this I asked Tom to spell *finance.* Again he produced it correctly and proceeded to spell, at my request, *financial* and *financially.* At this point I asked him why there was a *c* in *financial,* whereupon he observed that English spelling was crazy and did that kind of thing. So I wrote down the words *dance* and *place* and asked if the *c* was "crazy" there. He answered that that was all right and so was the *c* in *finance.* Then I asked again about the logic of *c* in *financial,* and the light began to dawn.

Tom then spelled *initial* correctly and then *initially.* Next he spelled *mission,* then *missionary; centrality,* then *central; existential* then *exist. Video* then *evidence* and, finally, *familiar* and *family,* which in Virginia dialect is pronounced "famly."

Altogether the "experiment" advanced as expected. Tom had learned well in elementary school, but the "sleepy years" had set in; he did little reading and writing, and little was demanded of him. During this same time, the grand vocabulary of abstraction had come under his command, but he had not examined it much in written form and his conscious intuition was to simply spell it by sound. The results, as we saw, were disastrous. Our one session had not cured his difficulties, but I think a right beginning was made. Moreover, I think many children in the middle and high school years would delight in this kind of word study and profit from it greatly.

In every form of language instruction, remedial or developmental, the return to basics must be a return to that basic tacit knowledge of the learner that is sound and firmly held. Effective teaching will depend on our ability to identify this knowledge truly and to exercise it rigorously.

Conclusions

Now it is time to bring my report to a close. I will do so by declaring some general conclusions that I have reached about the teaching of reading and writing in our world today. The first of these has to do with our culture as a whole.

Reading failure and illiteracy stem in largest part from cultural causes. All conditions that reduce the value of written language for individuals will tend to make its mastery unlikely, regardless of our educational efforts. How we will cope with a problem of this dimension I do not really know, but I believe that in some measure it must stem from a new regard for human difference and worth and the value of the written word.

It does seem to me that western thought in general has tended to view man as a superior animal whose destiny admits some ultimate control of the universe. It has followed from this, I think, that he who controls most is the highest valued. In the schoolroom today this is exemplified in the ubiquitous test of intelligence. Through the stark office of the normal curve, half of the human population is deemed worthless, another third ordinary, with but a gifted few admired.

It does seem to me that our posture on this matter is wrong in many ways and at many levels of thought. To begin with I am inclined to doubt that man is so altogether deserving as we have tended to think, though being one I cannot help but root rather strongly for him. At any event, I am convinced that our ability to manipulate affairs to advantage is circumscribed by the material given. No advancement can be made through waste, and I believe this must hold equally for our human as for our physical resources. To redirect our course so that we can achieve some viable standard of conservation will be an incredibly difficult undertaking, yet I suspect that our survival will depend on it.

In the schoolhouse, more conservative goals can be reached if society will permit us to do so. Barring gross injury and abnormality, nearly every child can learn to read and write in a manner appropriate to his needs and apprehensions. Education can compose a climate in which literacy is possible at least for those whose circumstance makes school attendance possible. To do so, however, norms and standards must be wholly revised and reinterpreted. We must learn to accept precocity with greater composure and the "less ripe-witted children" with greater optimism, love, and value. This would be such an easy and natural thing to do if we would but frame our minds to it. Within the sphere of education itself the major cause of reading failure stems from inappropriate teaching spurred by the false criteria derived from norms.

The drive for high achievement combined with technological systems of programmed skills has led in recent years to a massive withdrawal of children from reading and writing to some purpose. It has led also to a withdrawal of the teacher from the child and from an examination of the process of learning to read. To a frightening degree our curricula have become as dreary as the thumpings of a Coca-Cola bottling plant. Just the other day I saw an older man working a garden. As I watched, I suddenly realized that his handling of the spade was a thing of vast skill and artistry. I wish that something as fine as that might happen in our schools. If we could but develop a taste for such quality, I do think that literacy would thrive.

It has been my good fortune to study among professors and with students who have shared in great measure my own sense of what it is that education can and ought to do. It has been from this perspective that we have tried to look beyond the surface of skills toward the use of written language and the inner knowledge that allows children gradually to become literate. Our work of the past decade has provided me with some new and, I think, very practical insights about the specific character of this knowledge of English words. I have tried to show the origin of our efforts and how I think our findings may best be composed into a program of reading instruction in contemporary schools. These are not the only way to teach, nor have I given a cure to all educational ills, but this I do conclude. Our citizens should be better informed about reading and how it is learned so they can face honestly those heavy cultural imperatives that impinge upon it. Administrators must learn the same so that they can begin to revise the sad wreckage that normative teaching produces. The myth of learning disability must be dispelled, and "special education" confined to that which in fact is special. Finally, teachers must be freed from the blinding influence of prepared programs and educated to a deeper understanding of children and language. So armed, their humane tendencies, their wit and wisdom will make our schools anew—not as factories but as gardens of a flourishing civilization.

References

Allington, R. 1980. Poor readers don't get much in reading groups. *Language Arts*, *57*(8):872–76.

Almy, Millie C. 1966. *Young children's thinking: Studies of some aspects of Piaget's theory*. New York: Teachers College Press, Columbia University.

Anderson, R. C. 1977. *Schema-directed processes in language comprehension*. ERIC Document Reproduction Service No. ED 142977.

Ashton-Warner, Sylvia. 1963. *Teacher*. New York: Simon and Schuster.

Austin, Mary; and Morrison, Coleman. 1961. *The torch lighters: Tomorrow's teachers of reading*. Cambridge, Mass.: Harvard University Graduate School of Education. Distributed by Harvard University Press.

Ausubel, David P. 1960. The use of advance organizers in the learning and retention of meaningful verbal materials. *Journal of Educational Psychology*, *51*:267–72.

Bannatyne, Alexander. 1971. *Language, reading and learning disabilities*. Springfield, Ill.: Charles C Thomas.

Baugh, Albert C. 1957. *A history of the English language*. 2d ed. New York: Appleton-Century-Crofts.

Beers, Carol S. 1976. The relationship of conservation attainment to reading performance in second graders. Unpublished Ph.D. dissertation, University of Virginia.

Beers, J. 1974. First and second grade children's developing orthographic concepts of tense and lax vowels. Unpublished Ph.D. dissertation, University of Virginia.

Beers, J.; and Henderson, E. 1977. A study of developing orthographic concepts among first grade children. *Journal of Research in English*, *11*:133–48.

Beers, J. et al. 1977. Logic behind children's spellings. *Elementary School Journal*, *77*:238–42.

Bellugi, Ursula; and Brown, Roger, eds. 1964. *The acquisition of language*. Chicago: The University of Chicago Press.

Bereiter, Carl; and Engelmann, Siegfried. 1966. *Teaching disadvantaged children in preschool*. Englewood Cliffs, New Jersey: Prentice-Hall.

Berko, J. 1958. The child's learning of English morphology. *Word. 14*: 150–77.

Betts, Emmett Albert. 1946. *Foundations of reading instruction, with emphasis on differentiated guidance*. New York: American Book Co.

Bloomfield, Leonard. 1933. *Language*. New York: H. Holt and Co.

Bloomfield, L.; and Barnhart, Clarence L. 1963. *Let's read*. Bronxville, New York: Clarence L. Barnhart, Inc.

Bradley, Henry. 1918. On the relations between spoken and written language, with special reference to English. *Proceedings of the British Academy*. Vol. 6. London: Oxford University Press.

Brown, Roger W. 1973. *A first language: The early stages*. Cambridge, Mass.: Harvard University Press.

Bruner, J. S. 1960. *The process of education*. Cambridge, Mass.: Harvard University Press.

Bruner, J. S.; Goodnow, Jacqueline J.; and Austin, George A. 1956. *A study of thinking*. New York: John Wiley and Sons.

Bruner, J. S.; and Postman, L. 1947. Emotional selectivity in perception and reaction. *Journal of Personality*, 16:69–77.

Buchanan, Cynthia D.; and Sullivan Associates. 1963. *Programmed reading*. New York: McGraw-Hill.

Cahen, L.; Craun, M.; and Johnson, S. 1971. Spelling difficulty—A survey of the research. *Review of Educational Research*, 41: 281–301.

Calfee, R. C. 1972. Diagnostic evaluation of visual, auditory and general language factors in pre-readers. Paper presented at a meeting of the American Psychological Association. Honolulu, 1972.

Carrier, J. 1977. Social influence on the development of scientific knowledge: The case of learning disability. Unpublished Ph.D. dissertation, London School of Economics.

Carroll, John B. 1965. *Some neglected relationships in reading and language learning*. Paper presented at the 55th Convention of the National Council of Teachers of English, Boston, 1965.

Carroll, John B. 1972. Review of the ITPA. In *The seventh mental measurements yearbook*, edited by Oscar Krisen Buros, Highland Park, New Jersey: The Gryphon Press.

Chall, Jeanne. 1967. *Learning to read: The great debate*. New York: McGraw-Hill.

Chomsky, C. 1970. Reading, writing, and phonology. *Harvard Educational Review*, 40(2):287–309.

Chomsky, C. 1971. Write first, read later. *Childhood Education*, 47: 269–99.

Chomsky, C. 1972. Stages in language development and language exposure. *Harvard Educational Review*, 42(1):1–33.

Chomsky, C. 1976. Approaching reading through invented spelling. Paper presented at the Conference on Theory and Practice of Beginning Reading Instruction, Learning Research and Development Center, University of Pittsburgh, May 1976.

Chomsky, N. 1957. *Syntactic structures*. The Hague: Mouton.

Chomsky, N. 1959. Review of Skinner's *Verbal Behavior*. *Language*, 35:26–58.

Chomsky, N. 1965. *Aspects of the theory of syntax*. Cambridge, Mass.: MIT Press.

Chomsky, N. 1966. *Cartesian linguistics*. New York: Harper and Row.

Chomsky, N. 1968. *Language and mind*. New York: Harcourt, Brace, and World.

Chomsky, N. 1970. Phonology and reading. In *Basic studies in reading*, edited by H. Levin and J. P. Williams. New York: Basic Books.

Chomsky, N. 1975. *Reflections on language*. New York: Pantheon Books.

Chomsky, N.; and Halle, M. 1968. *The sound pattern of English*. New York: Harper and Row.

Clay, Marie M. 1976. Early childhood and cultural diversity in New Zealand. *The Reading Teacher, 29*(4):333–42.

Cruickshank, W. M.; Bentzen, Frances A.; Ratzeburg, Frederick H.; and Tannhauser, Miriam T. 1961. *A teaching method for brain-injured and hyperactive children*. Syracuse University Special Education and Rehabilitation Monograph Series 6. Syracuse, N.Y.: Syracuse University Press.

Davis, Frederick B. 1944. Fundamental factors of comprehension in reading. *Psychometrika, 9*(3):185–97.

De Beaugrande, R. 1981. Design criteria for process models of reading. *Reading Research Quarterly, 16*(2):261–315.

DeCecco, J. P. 1967. *The psychology of language, thought and instruction*. New York: Holt, Rinehart, and Winston.

Deese, James Earle. 1970. *Psycholinguistics*. Boston: Allyn and Bacon.

Dewey, J. 1933. *How we think: A restatement of the relation of reflective thinking to the educative process*. New York: D. C. Heath and Co.

Downing, John; and Oliver, Peter. 1973–1974. The child's conception of "a word." *Reading Research Quarterly, 9*(4):568–82.

Dzama, Mary Ann. 1972. A comparative study of natural vs. frequency control sight vocabularies on the basis of forty-five phonic generalizations. Unpublished Ph.D. dissertation, University of Virginia.

Eccles, John C. 1977. *The understanding of the brain*. 2d ed. New York: McGraw-Hill.

Elkind, D. 1970. *Children and adolescents: Interpretive essays on Jean Piaget*. New York: Oxford University Press.

Elkind, D. 1974. Cognitive development and reading. Paper presented at the Annual Convention of the International Reading Association, New Orleans, 1974.

Fernald, Grace Maxwell. 1943. *Remedial techniques in basic school subjects*. New York: McGraw-Hill.

Fisher, E. 1973. A linguistic investigation of first grade children's spelling errors as they occur in their written compositions. Unpublished Ph.D. dissertation, University of Virginia.

Flavell, J. H. 1963. *The developmental psychology of Jean Piaget*. Princeton: J. J. Nostrand.

Flesch, Rudolph. 1955. *Why Johnny can't read—and what you can do about it*. New York: Harper.

Frederickson, Carl H. 1975. Acquisition of semantic information from discourse: Effects of repeated exposures. *Journal of Verbal Learning and Verbal Behavior, 14*:158–69.

Fries, Charles. 1962. *Linguistics and reading*. New York: Holt, Rinehart, and Winston.

Frith, U. 1980. Unexpected spelling problems. In *Cognitive processes in spelling*. New York: Academic Press, pp. 495–515.

Frostig, M.; and Horne, David. 1964. *The Frostig program for the development of visual perception*. Chicago: Follett Educational Corp.

Fuller, Renee. 1974. Severely retarded people can learn to read. *Psychology Today*, 8(5):96–102.

Gates, A. 1936. *A list of spelling difficulties in 3,876 words*. New York: Columbia University Press.

Gattegno, Caleb. 1964. *Words in color*. Chicago: Encyclopaedia Britannica, Inc.

Gentry, J. R. 1977a. A study of the orthographic strategies of beginning readers. Unpublished Ph.D. dissertation, University of Virginia.

Gentry, J. R. 1977b. Three steps to teaching beginning readers to spell. A paper presented at the Twenty-Second Annual Convention of the International Reading Association, Miami, May 1977.

Gentry, J. R.; and Henderson, E. H. 1980. Three steps to teaching beginning readers to spell. In *Developmental and cognitive aspects of learning to spell*, edited by E. H. Henderson and J. Beers. Newark, Delaware: International Reading Association.

Geschwind, Norman. 1974. *Selected papers on language and the brain*. Boston Studies in the Philosophy of Science, Vol. 16, edited by Robert S. Cohen and Mark W. Wartofsky. Boston: D. Reidel Publishing Co.

Gesell, Arnold. 1940. *The first five years of life*. New York: Harper.

Getzels, Jacob W.; and Jackson, Phillip W. 1962. *Creativity and intelligence: Explorations with gifted students*. New York: John Wiley and Sons.

Gibson, E. 1965. Learning to read. *Science, 148*:1066–72.

Gibson, E. 1969. *Principles of perceptual learning and development*. New York: Appleton-Century-Crofts.

Gibson, E. 1970. The ontogeny of reading. *American Psychologist, 25*(2):136–45.

Gibson, E. J.; and Levin, H. 1975. *The psychology of reading*. Cambridge, Mass.: MIT Press.

Gleitman, L. R.; and Rozin, P. 1973. Teaching reading by use of a syllabary. *Reading Research Quarterly, 8*:447–83.

Gleitman, L. R.; and Rozin, P. 1977. The structure and acquisition of reading 1: Relations between orthographics and the structure of language. In *Toward a psychology of reading*. Proceedings of the CUNY Conferences. New York: John Wiley and Sons.

Goldschmid, M.; and Bentler, P. 1968. *Concept assessment kit—Conservation*. California: Educational and Industrial Testing Service.

Goodman, K. 1976. Reading: A psycholinguistic guessing game. In *Theoretical models and processes of reading*, edited by H. Singer and R. Ruddell. 2d ed. Newark, Delaware: International Reading Association, pp. 497–508.

Goodman, Yetta M.; and Burke, Carolyn L. 1972. *Reading miscue inventory manual: Procedure for diagnosis and evaluation*. New York: Macmillan Co.

Gough, P. 1972. One second of reading. In *Language by ear and by eye*, edited by J. Kavanagh and I. Mattingly. Cambridge, Mass.: MIT Press.

Gray, William S.; Marion, Monroe A.; and Sterl, Artley, et al. 1956. *The new basic reading program.* Curriculum Foundation Series. Chicago: Scott, Foresman and Co.

Guilford, J. P. 1959. Three faces of intellect, *American Psychologist,* *14*:469–79.

Hammill, Donald D.; Goodman, Libby; and Wiederbolt, J. L. 1974. Visual motor processes: Can we train them? *The Reading Teacher,* *27*(5):469–78.

Hammill, Donald D.; and Larsen, Stephen C. 1974. The effectiveness of psycholinguistic training. *Exceptional Children,* *41*:5–14.

Hanna, P. R.; Hanna, J. S.; Hodges, R. E.; and Rudorf, E. H. 1966. *Phoneme-grapheme correspondences as cues to spelling improvement.* Washington, D.C.: U.S. Government Printing Office.

Hanna, P. R.; and Moore, J. T. 1953. Spelling—from spoken word to written symbol. *Elementary School Journal,* 53:329–37.

Harris, Theodore; Creekmore, Mildred; Mattean, Louisa; and Allen, Harold B. 1960. *Keys to reading.* Oklahoma City: The Economy Co., reprinted, 1975.

Hays, W. 1965. *Statistics for psychologists.* New York: Holt, Rinehart, and Winston.

Heatherly, Anna L. 1972. Attainment of Piagetian conservation tasks. Unpublished Ph.D. dissertation, University of Virginia.

Henderson, E.; and Beers, J., eds. 1980. *Developmental and cognitive aspects of learning to spell: A reflection of word knowledge.* Newark, Delaware: International Reading Association.

Henderson, E.; Estes, T. H.; and Stonecash, S. 1972. An exploratory study of word acquisition among first graders at mid-year in a language experience approach. *Journal of Reading Behavior,* 4: 21–30.

Hermann, K.; and Norrie, E. 1958. Is congenital word-blindness a hereditary type of Gerstmann's syndrome? *Psychiat. Neurol.* (Basel) *136*:59.

Hoole, Charles. 1969. *A new discovery of the old art of teaching school, 1960.* Menston, Yorkshire, England: Scolar Press, Ltd.

Horn, Ernest. 1937. *Methods of instruction in the social studies.* New York: Scribner's.

Horn, Thomas D. 1957. Phonetics and spelling. *Elementary School Journal,* *57*:424–32.

Howes, Davis. 1962. An approach to the quantitative analysis of word blindness. In *Reading disability,* edited by John Money. Baltimore: The Johns Hopkins University Press, 1962.

Huey, E. B. 1908. *The psychology and pedagogy of reading.* New York: Macmillan Co.

Hull, Clark L.; Howland, Carl I.; Ross, Robert T., et al. 1940. *Mathematico-deductive theory of rote learning: A study in scientific methodology.* New Haven, Conn.: Yale University Press.

Hunt, J. McVicker. 1961. *Intelligence and experience.* New York: Ronald Press Co.

Hunt, Lyman C. 1952. A further study of certain factors associated with reading comprehension. Unpublished Ph.D. dissertation, Syracuse University.

Jacobson, Milton D. 1974. Predicting reading difficulty from spelling. *The Spelling Progress Bulletin*, Spring pp. 8–10.

James, W. 1899. *Talks to teachers on psychology, and to students of some of life's ideals*. Reprinted, New York: W. W. Norton and Co., 1958.

Kavanagh, J.; and Venezky, R. 1980. *Orthography, reading and dyslexia*. Baltimore: University Park Press.

Kephart, N. C. 1971. *The slow learner in the classroom*. 2d ed. Columbus, Ohio: Charles E. Merrill.

Kintch, W. 1974. *The representation of meaning in memory*. Hillsdale, New Jersey: Lawrence Erlbaum Associates.

Kirk, Samuel Alexander. 1971. *Educating exceptional children*. 2d ed. Boston: Houghton Mifflin.

Kuhn, T. 1970. *The structure of scientific revolutions*. Chicago: The University of Chicago Press.

Lashley, Karl Spencer. 1929. *Brain mechanisms and intelligence: A quantitative study of injuries to the brain*. Chicago: The University of Chicago Press.

Laurendeau, Monique; and Pinard, Adrian. 1968. *Causal thinking in the child: A genetic and experimental approach*. New York: International Universities Press.

Lavine, L. O. 1975. The development of perception of writing in pre-reading children: A cross-cultural study. Unpublished Ph.D. dissertation, Cornell University.

LaBerge, D.; and Samuels, S. J. 1974. Toward a theory of automatic information processing in reading. *Cognitive Psychology*, 6: 293–323.

Lennon, Roger T. 1962. What can be measured? *The Reading Teacher*, 15(5):326–37.

Liberman, I. 1973. Segmentation of the spoken word and reading acquisition. Paper presented at the Society for Research and Child Development. Philadelphia, March 1973.

Lieberman, Philip. 1975. *On the origins of language: An introduction to the evolution of human speech*. New York: Macmillan Co.

Lyons, J. 1970. *Noam Chomsky*. New York: The Viking Press.

MacNemar, Quinn. 1964. Lost: Our intelligence? Why? *American Psychologist*, 19(12):871–72.

Mazurkiewicz, Albert J.; and Tanzer, Harold J. 1963. *Early to read: i t a program*. New York: Initial Teaching Alphabet Publications, Inc.

McAdam, E. L.; and Milne, G. 1963. *Johnson's Dictionary: A modern selection*. New York: Harper Colophon Books.

McCall, W. A.; and Crabbs, L. H. 1961. *Standard test lessons in reading*. New York: Teachers College Press, Columbia University.

McGuffey, William Holmes. 1866. *McGuffey's new first-sixth eclectic reader*. New York: Van Antwerp, Brass and Co.

Mehegan, Charles C.; and Dreifuss, Fritz E. 1972. Hyperlexia: Exceptional reading ability in brain-damaged children. *Neurology* *22*(11):1105–1111.

Menyuk, P. 1968. Children's learning and production of grammatical and nongrammatical sequences. *Child Development, 39*:849–59.

Moore, Samuel. 1951. Historical outline at English pathology and middle grammar. Revised by Albert H. Marckwardt. Ann Arbor, Mich.: George Wahr.

Morris, D. 1979. Some aspects of the instructional environment and learning to read. *Language Arts, 56*(5):475–502.

Morris, D. 1980. Beginning reader's concept of word and its relation to phoneme segmentation ability. Unpublished Ph.D. dissertation, University of Virginia.

Morris, D. 1980. Beginning reader's concept of word. In *Developmental and cognitive aspects of learning to spell*, edited by E. Henderson and J. Beers. Newark, Delaware: International Reading Association.

Moskowitz, B. A. 1973. On the status of vowel shift in English. In *Cognitive development and the acquisition of language*, edited by T. Moore. New York: Academic Press, pp. 223–60.

Ogden, C.; and Richards, I. 1946. *The meaning of meaning.* New York: Harcourt, Brace, and World.

Orton, Samuel Torrey. 1937. *Reading, writing and speech problems in children: A presentation of certain types of disorders in the development of the language faculty.* New York: W. W. Norton.

Otto, Wayne; and Askov, Eunice. 1970. *The Wisconsin design for reading skill development: Rationale and guidelines.* Minneapolis: National Computer Systems.

Papandropoulou, I.; and Sinclair, H. 1974. What is a word? Experimental study of children's ideas on grammar. *Human Development, 17*:241–58.

Paraskevopoulos, John N.; and Kirk, Samuel A. 1969. *The development and psychometric characteristics of the revised Illinois test of psycholinguistic abilities.* Champaign, Ill.: University of Illinois Press.

Piaget, Jean. 1967. Cognitions and conservations. Two views. *Contemporary Psychology, 12*:532–33.

Pitman, Sir James; and St. John, John. 1969. *Alphabets and reading: The initial teaching alphabet.* New York: Pitman Learning Inc.

Rappaport, Sheldon R. 1964. Narbeth, Penn.: The Pathway School.

Read, C. 1970. Children's perceptions of the sounds of English: Phonology from 3–6. Unpublished Ph.D. dissertation, Harvard University.

Read, C. 1971. Pre-school children's knowledge of English phonology. *Harvard Educational Review, 41*:1–34.

Read, C. 1975. *Children's categorization of speech sounds in English.* Urbana, Ill.: National Council of Teachers of English.

Read, C. 1976. Paper presented before the National Reading Conference, Atlanta, December 1976.

Reed, D. W. 1976. A review by a specialist in dialectology. *Research in the Teachings of English, 1*:207–15.

Roberts, A. 1967. A review by a specialist in the uses of computers in linguistic research. *Research in the Teaching of English*, 1: 201–7.

Robinson, Francis P. 1961. *Effective study*. New York: Harper and Row.

Sapir, E. 1925. Sound patterns in language. *Language*, 1:37–51.

Scragg, D. 1974. *A history of English spelling*. London: Manchester University Press.

Skinner, B. F. 1957. *Verbal behavior*. New York: Appleton-Century-Crofts.

Smith, F. 1971. *Understanding reading*. New York: Holt, Rinehart and Winston.

Smith, Nila Banton. 1965. *American reading instruction: Its development and its significance in gaining a perspective on current practices in reading*. Newark, Delaware: International Reading Association.

Smith, Phillip G.; and Hullfish, Henry G. 1961. *Reflective thinking: The method of education*. New York: Dodd, Mead.

Stauffer, R. G. 1970. *The language-experience approach to the teaching of reading*. New York: Harper and Row.

Stever, E. F. 1976. Dialectic and socioeconomic factors affecting the spelling strategies of second grade students. Unpublished Ph.D. dissertation, University of Virginia.

Strauss, Alfred A. 1955. *Psychopathology and education of the brain-impaired child*. New York: Grune and Stratton.

Swadesh, M.; and Voegelin, C. F. 1939. A problem in phonological alteration. *Language*, 15:1–10.

Temple, C. 1978. An analysis of spelling errors from Gates 1936. Unpublished M.S. thesis, University of Virginia.

Templeton, S. 1976. An awareness of certain aspects of derivational morphology in phonology and orthography among sixth, eighth, and tenth graders. Unpublished Ph.D. dissertation, University of Virginia.

Templeton, S. 1980. Circle game of English spelling: A reappraisal for teachers. *Language Arts*, 56:789–97.

Thorndike, Edward L.; and Lorge, Irving. 1944. *The teacher's word book of 30,000 words*. New York: Teachers College Press, Columbia University.

Thorndike, Robert L. 1973–1974. Reading as reasoning. *Reading Research Quarterly*, 9(2):135–47.

Thurstone, L. L. 1946. Note on a reanalysis of Davis' reading tests. *Psychometrika*, 11(8):185–88.

Torrance, E. Paul; and Gupta, Ram. 1964. *Development and evaluation of recorded programmed experiences in creative thinking in the fourth grade*. Minneapolis: Bureau of Educational Research, College of Education, University of Minnesota.

Trace, Arthur S. 1961. *What Ivan knows that Johnny doesn't*. New York: Random House.

Vallins, G. 1973. *Spelling*. Revised by D. G. Scragg. London: Andre Deutsch.

Venezky, R. L. 1967. English orthography: Its graphical structure and its relation to sound. *Reading Research Quarterly*, 2(3):75–105.

Weimer, W. 1973. Psycholinguistics and Plato's paradoxes of the Meno. *American Psychologist*, 15–31.

Wheeler, D. D. 1970. Processes in word recognition. *Cognitive Psychology*, 1:59–85.

White, Burton L.; and Watts, Jean Carew. 1973. *Experience and environment: Major influences on the development of the young child.* Vol. 1. Englewood Cliffs, New Jersey: Prentice-Hall.

Zutell, J. 1975. Spelling strategies of primary school children and their relationships to the Piagetian concept of decentration. Unpublished Ph.D. dissertation, University of Virginia.

Zutell, J. 1980. Children's spelling strategies and their cognitive development. In *Developmental and cognitive aspects of learning to spell*, edited by E. Henderson and J. Beers. Newark, Delaware: International Reading Association.